"T   pply market   valuable
in   velop the
pro   d for our
mir   face and
giv   sponsible
and

Syl
Ch
Ch
Di

"L   marketing
cle   tion exec-
uti   a big step
for   ency. The
bo   ws how to
use   the King-
do

Steve Woodworth, MBA
Vice President of Marketing
World Vision, Inc.

Marketing for Churches and Ministries

HAWORTH Marketing Resources:
Innovations in Practice & Professional Services
William J. Winston, Senior Editor

New, Recent, and Forthcoming Titles:

Long Term Care Administration: The Management of Institutional and Non-Institutional Components of the Continuum of Care by Ben Abramovice

Cases and Select Readings in Health Care Marketing, edited by Robert E. Sweeney, Robert L. Berl, and William J. Winston

Marketing Planning Guide by Robert E. Stevens, David L. Loudon, and William E. Warren

Marketing for Churches and Ministries by Robert E. Stevens and David L. Loudon

The Clinician's Guide to Managed Mental Health Care by Norman Winegar

Professional Services Marketing: Strategy and Tactics by F. G. Crane

A Guide to Preparing Cost-Effective Press Releases by Robert H. Loeffler

How to Create Interest-Evoking, Sales-Inducing, Non-Irritating Advertising by Walter Weir

Market Analysis: Assessing Your Business Opportunities by Robert E. Stevens, Philip K. Sherwood, and J. Paul Dunn

Marketing for Churches and Ministries

Robert E. Stevens, MBA, PhD
David L. Loudon, MBA, PhD

The Haworth Press
New York • London • Norwood (Australia)

The Haworth Press, Inc., 10 Alice Street, Binghamton, NY 13904-1580

Library of Congress Cataloging-in-Publication Data

Stevens, Robert E., 1942-
    Marketing for churches and ministries / Robert E. Stevens and David L. Loudon.
        p. cm.
    Includes bibliographic references and index.
    ISBN 1-56024-177-2 **ISBN 1-56024-593-X (PBK.)**
    1. Church publicity. I. Loudon, David L. II. Title.
BV653.S815 1992
254.4 — dc20
                                                                                91-4069
                                                                                CIP

CONTENTS

ABOUT THE AUTHORS

Robert E. Stevens, MBA, PhD, is Professor of Marketing in the College of Business Administration at Northeast Louisiana University in Monroe, Louisiana. He is the author of eight books and more than 65 articles dealing with marketing and its application to various areas. Dr. Stevens has served as a consultant to local, regional, and national firms for research projects, feasibility studies, and marketing planning, and was a partner in a marketing research company for three years prior to moving to Louisiana. He also taught for ten years at Oral Roberts University where he was active in marketing projects for the university and ministry. Dr. Stevens is a member of the Southwest Marketing Association, the Southern Marketing Association, and the Atlantic Marketing Association.

David L. Loudon, MBA, PhD, is Professor of Marketing and Head of the Department of Management and Marketing in the College of Business Administration at Northeast Louisiana University in Monroe, Louisiana. He is the author of numerous articles and books on consumer behavior and legal services marketing. Dr. Loudon has conducted research in the United States, Europe, and Latin America on a variety of topics, including the application of marketing concepts to nontraditional areas. He has served as a consultant to numerous organizations and is president of a computer software firm. Dr. Loudon is also a member of the Southwest Marketing Association, the Southern Marketing Association, the Atlantic Marketing Association, and the American Marketing Association.

Preface

Marketing has come of age for many nonprofit organizations in recent years. This is evidenced by the large number of publications aimed at those organizations. Journals as well as books on marketing of health care, education and professional services attest to the growing recognition of the application of marketing to many nontraditional and nonbusiness areas. However, one area where only limited published application of marketing exists is for churches and ministries. We believe that no organization or group has a message of such urgent and life-changing content as the message of faith in God. Yet most churches fail to use the concepts and tools which can enable them to effectively communicate to current and prospective members and donors, as well as other groups which need so desperately to hear this message.

Our book in no way alters or intends to alter the message a minister proclaims nor will the book try to make a minister a "polished salesman." These are common misconceptions of what marketing involves and will be identified as fallacies in Chapter 1 of the book. Our book will clearly show how marketing concepts and techniques can be used to effectively meet the needs of a church's or ministry's constituents.

The book was written from a practical standpoint and includes numerous examples of the use of marketing concepts and tools. It also includes sample marketing plans in an appendix to demonstrate what an actual plan entails. The book is both theoretically sound and practically oriented. Each chapter ends with worksheets to enable readers to develop their own marketing plan as they proceed through the book.

Acknowledgments

A book is seldom the work of the authors alone, but reflects inputs from many sources. We would especially like to express our appreciation to the following people: Jason Swain, Shari Humphrey, and Diane Mathevosian for their help in preparing drafts of examples and marketing plans; Rev. Mickey Humphrey, Senior Pastor of Pine Grove Church in Monroe, Louisiana and Rev. Bob Clanton, Monroe Covenant Church in Monroe, Louisiana for encouragement and insights into church marketing problems; Rev. Edgar Stone for use in the book of the marketing plan for his Mexico mission work.

We also want to express our appreciation to Melba Cheek, Terrie Harris, Shea Pardue, and Rebecca Ross for typing the many drafts of the book. Finally, special thanks to Dr. Henry Migliore who encouraged us to write this book.

Chapter 1

Understanding Church and Ministry Marketing

Marketing in Action

A recent survey of 190 clergy of various denominations and 261 of the general public measured their views on the appropriateness of church marketing activities. The study revealed that the clergy is more positive than the general public toward church use of marketing activities. The most commonly used marketing activity was a regular listing in the yellow pages.

The two groups were asked to rank forty-three marketing activities as appropriate or inappropriate for a church. These forty-three activities could be grouped into five categories:

1. Service offering and design
2. Distribution
3. Promotion
4. Pricing
5. Market research

The activities viewed most appropriate by both groups were the "distribution" activities (i.e., providing free transportation, broadcasting church services on radio and television). The "pricing" activity, for example, special programs designed to encourage members to increase their monetary giving to the church, was viewed by the general public as not favorable. "Promotion" activities, such as personal visits and personal acknowledgement of visitors, were viewed as more appropriate than nonpersonal promotion (advertising). The clergy viewed "marketing research" activities (e.g., formal surveys) as more appropriate than did the general public. The survey provided some interesting results concerning "service offering design" activities. Both the clergy and general public favorably

viewed special programs that provided social and service organizations for members of the church. At the same time, the updating of
church doctrine and updating the church's view on acceptable behavior for individuals is viewed negatively by the clergy, but more
positively by the general public. The overall results from this study
indicate that the general public and clergy are becoming more positive toward church marketing activities.[1]

More and more public and private nonprofit organization administrators are attending marketing seminars, reading marketing literature and discussing marketing topics at internal meetings.[2] They
want to know how they can use marketing in their own organizations as they face increasingly difficult problems in their operations.
Churches and ministries are no exception. They want to know how
advertising, public relations, fund raising, planning and promotion
are all related to marketing.

Churches and ministries face a number of problems which would
be treated as marketing problems if they were found in the business
sector. Churches and ministries are having difficulty attracting and
maintaining active members/supporters; they are having difficulty
determining if they are meeting these people's needs; and they are
unable to explain why members and supporters leave or stop supporting their organizations. In many instances they suffer from poor
images or just a lack of knowledge about how to effectively communicate what their organization is and the ways in which it could
serve people. There are not many churches or ministries that don't
have some problems that stem from their relationships with their
constituents.

WHAT IS MARKETING?

What is marketing and how can it help an organization? Marketing, as used in this book, is the management of an organization's
exchanges with its various constituents. A constituent is someone
who works for, is a member of, attends, supports, or is affected by
an organization.

Most people really do not understand marketing and view it as
selling, advertising or public relations. This is readily understand-

able when you consider the large number of television and radio commercials a person is exposed to every day. It is often surprising to administrators to discover that selling and advertising are only a part of marketing.

In today's environment, churches and ministries must know how to analyze their constituents' needs, attract resources, and use these resources to develop the programs, services and ideas which will attract and maintain their constituents.

In our definition of marketing, exchange is the central element. Two or more parties enter into an exchange for the mutual benefit of both parties. Each party has something of value to the other party and both parties are better off after the exchange than they were before the exchange took place. One party, a church or ministry, is offering something needed by the other party. The other party, constituents, enters into the exchange and has its needs met while at the same time meeting the needs of the church or ministry. (See Exhibit 1-1.)

A marketer is someone who has the knowledge and skills to understand, plan and manage exchanges. The marketer knows how to go about assessing constituents' needs, developing programs to meet these needs, and then effectively communicating what is offered to the constituents.

Now, given this background, let's redefine church and ministry marketing as it will be used throughout the remainder of this book:

Church/Ministry Marketing is the analysis, planning and management of voluntary exchanges between a church or ministry and its constituents for the purpose of satisfying the needs of both parties. It concentrates on the analysis of constituents'

EXHIBIT 1-1. The Exchange Process

needs, developing programs to meet these needs, providing these programs at the right time and place, communicating effectively with constituents, and attracting the resources needed to underwrite the activities of the organization.

Several things need to be emphasized in this definition. First, marketing is grounded in the analysis of the needs of constituents. A marketer does not concentrate on trying to "sell something," but rather identifying and providing for constituents' needs. This need-oriented approach is a fundamental difference between marketing and selling.

Second, marketing concentrates on exchanges that are mutually beneficial for both parties. It does not promote a "win-lose" philosophy, but a "win-win" philosophy in which both parties are better off for being involved in the exchange.

Third, marketing's focus is on carefully formulating programs, times, places, communications and funding activities in relation to the needs of constituents. In this sense, marketing is the response mechanism of the organization. As the needs of constituents change, programs, communication, funding, etc. must change.

Finally, marketing's focus is on the needs of an organization's constituents. The organization does not attempt to meet the needs of everyone, but only those constituents it is best equipped to serve. The doctrinal, denominational and local environment ensure that an organization cannot be all things to all people. Marketing helps an organization carefully identify who it wants to serve. Then the organization's activities are oriented to serve specific constituent groups which are identified through a marketing analysis.

THE ROLE OF MARKETING
IN CHURCHES AND MINISTRIES

A better focus of what marketing is capable of doing for an organization may be gained by an examination of Exhibit 1-2. This table illustrates different levels or stages of marketing orientation in an organization. When organizations have a program orientation, they are more concerned about doing things right than doing the right

EXHIBIT 1-2. Stages in the Development of Marketing Thought

ERA	THEME
1. Program orientation	How can we develop more programs?
2. Sales orientation	How can we get more people to attend our programs?
3. Marketing orientation	How can our activities be oriented toward the constituent?

things. The emphasis is on improving what they are currently doing.

A sales emphasis orients the organization toward constituents, but only tries to get them to participate in what is already offered. The emphasis is on building volume for the sake of volume. More is better under this concept.

The last stage of development begins when administrators start to realize that everyone needs to be concerned about constituents' needs. One management writer stated this idea succinctly when he said that the basic purpose or reason for existence for every organization is to create a customer or a constituent. The extension of this orientation, also known as the marketing concept, views the organization with the constituents' needs at the center of the organization. This does not in any way replace the idea that a church or ministry must be Christ-centered. It simply means that the spiritual needs of the members of a church or supporters of a ministry should determine the programs and services rendered by the organization.

Administrators operating under this philosophy must continually survey the environment to detect changes in constituent needs or other related variables that warrant altering the church/ministry's activities. Attendance and audience size, in effect, become votes to help administrators judge the effectiveness of their efforts in meeting needs. Putting this philosophy into practice requires a planning procedure that focuses on the needs of the people the organization is trying to serve.

The marketing concept orients organizational thinking toward the constituents to be served rather than programs or promotion of existing programs. This is the first step in developing a marketing organization. The second step involves identifying what constitutes marketing variables within an organization. Within a church/ministry setting, these variables are shown in Exhibit 1-3 below.

The needs of the organization's constituents become the focus of the programs offered by the church/ministry. Information about the nature of the organization and the programs offered is then communicated to these constituents. Constituents must have access to these programs at the right time and the right place in order for their needs to be met. Finally, contributions must be solicited from constituents to support the programs which are offered. Marketing concentrates on meeting the constituents' needs through providing the right programs, with the right communication, at the right time and place, and by generating the right level of contributions from constituents.

All this must be done within the context of the environment in which each church/ministry operates. Each organization has its own unique environment which is created by the community's religious environment, denominational affiliation (if any), community characteristics and any legal or political pressures which must be addressed. These environments directly affect what the church/ministry can do in altering its programs, communications, etc.; but they are beyond the control of a specific church or ministry and must be considered when evaluating old activities or starting new ones. For example, starting a church day care program would bring local, state and federal regulations to bear on the organization's activities because day care centers are regulated by various governmental agencies. Thus, complying with these regulations must be an influencing factor in designing the program.

EXHIBIT 1-3

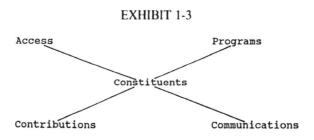

CRITICISMS AGAINST MARKETING

Marketing carries negative connotations in the minds of many people. Plato, Aristotle, Aquinas and other early philosophers thought of merchants as unproductive and acquisitive. Merchants were seen as taking advantage of helpless customers through buying "cheap" and selling "dear." In modern times, marketers are accused of getting people to buy what they do not want. Customers are often seen as victims.

Several professions—medicine, law, accounting—banned their licensed members from engaging in any explicit marketing activities in the pursuit of clients until recently. Their codes of professional ethics were interpreted to mean they should not be involved in direct client solicitation, advertising and price cutting. The practitioners were above "selling" their services. They were simply "available" to those who needed their help. However, the Supreme Court ruled that these bans had the effect of reducing competition by denying firms the right to inform potential clients about their services and to provide useful information. Marketing activities are now common in these professions.

Many other organizations come close to the professions in their negative attitude toward marketing. Many Christians feel that a church or ministry should not "sell" itself. In fact, three specific criticisms are often made against marketing activities.

Marketing Activities Waste Money

A frequent criticism of marketing activities is that they cost too much. For example, spending $2,000 a year for newspaper ads about church services may be seen as a waste of money, money that could have been spent on something "valuable."

Organizations, of course, should not add costs that do not produce a benefit to someone. They should not overspend, but they also should not underspend. Most churches/ministries are more prone to underspend than to overspend on marketing.

Marketing Activities Invade Privacy

A second objection to marketing activities is that they often intrude into people's personal lives. Marketing researchers ask people about their likes and dislikes, beliefs, attitudes, incomes and other personal matters. For example, one church passed out questionnaires to families during a service to collect data on children's ages, school enrollment, income, etc. Some people objected to the information being collected, but the purpose was to evaluate the need for a proposed church-related school. Data from this survey revealed that interest was not strong enough among members to pursue the school; thus, they avoided a costly mistake.

Marketing research is primarily carried on to learn the needs of constituents and their attitudes toward the organization's current programs so that the organization can deliver greater satisfaction to its constituents. At the same time, organizations must show a sensitivity to people's need for privacy.

Marketing Manipulates People

A third criticism is that organizations use marketing to manipulate people. This involves making people buy products they do not need or spend money they do not have. This is most likely to happen when the organization is pushing hard to get a program started or get funding for a new building project.

Administrators should be sensitive to the charge of manipulation when they implement a marketing program. In most cases, it is just a matter of people being overzealous in their desire to see results accomplished. In other cases, the charge is justified and such activities should be stopped to avoid actions and attitudes detrimental to the organization and to marketing in general.

MAJOR BENEFITS ASSOCIATED WITH MARKETING

The basic reason an organization should be interested in applying marketing principles is that they will enable it to achieve its objectives more effectively. Organizations in our country depend upon voluntary exchanges to accomplish their objectives. Marketing is the discipline concerned with managing exchanges effectively and efficiently.

Marketing produces three major benefits for the organization and its constituents.

Improved Satisfaction of Constituents

Many organizations lack the tools needed to satisfy their constituents and may deliver unsatisfactory services which people accept because there are no alternatives. In many instances, administrators simply do not know how to improve on what they are currently offering. Marketing, which focuses on the importance of measuring and satisfying constituent needs, tends to produce an improved level of service and satisfaction.

Improved Attraction of Resources

Organizations, in striving to satisfy a set of constituents, must attract various resources, including members, volunteers, employees, funds and, sometimes, public support. Marketing provides an approach to improving the organization's ability to attract needed resources.

Improved Efficiency of Activities

Marketing places a great emphasis on rational management and coordination of programs, contributions, communication and access. Many organizations make these decisions with insufficient knowledge, resulting in either more cost for the given impact or less impact for the given cost. The scarcity of funds in most churches and ministries means that the maximum results must be achieved per dollar of expenditure.

Marketing's focus on the coordination of activities and concentration on constituents' needs usually produces more efficient efforts from activities. (If constituents receive the right communications, the amount of wasted funds can be reduced.) Marketing aids in identifying what the right messages are and, therefore, improves efficiency.

MARKETING PITFALLS

Many administrators, convinced that the benefits of marketing outweigh the criticisms, may subject themselves to one of many pitfalls related to attitudes toward marketing. These pitfalls are identified and discussed below to help avoid these damages.

Pitfall 1: Good marketing can make up for poor performance elsewhere in the organization. This attitude leads to the idea that poorly planned programs, poor selection of teaching topics, poor delivery of sermons and poorly planned activities can be smoothed out or covered up by using the proper marketing techniques. This is not the intent of marketing, and certainly proves fruitless in the long run. No matter how well we communicate, research, provide easy access, etc. — poor sermons are still poor sermons. In fact, an organization should not promise more than it can deliver — because constituents will surely be disappointed.

Pitfall 2: Now that we are using the marketing framework for decision making, we can always make decisions based on what constituents need or say they need. This attitude preempts the Lordship of the Holy Spirit to work through pastors, teachers and other ministry personnel. Most members of a given congregation may not feel the need to fast, for example, yet the Lord may lead a pastor to call for a churchwide fast. Marketing, if viewed properly, in no way replaces the inspiration, guidance and leadership that a minister or administrator receives from God. If a church operates as a "New Testament Church," then the New Testament is a guide to what should/should not happen in the church — not the whims of a "fickle" people who may want what they do not need and need what they do not want!

Pitfall 3: Somehow it is not spiritual to use the same techniques a business uses in a religious setting. Again, if marketing is properly used, this pitfall can be avoided. If our church installs a sound system just like the one used by a rock group or a theater, are we unspiritual? What about the use of lights, vans, painted signs, and photocopied music sheets? Aren't these also used by businesses? This pitfall is akin to the often misquoted scripture that "money is the root of all evil." The scripture actually says "the *love* of money is the root of all evil." Money is not good or bad in itself; but our attitude toward money and how we use it can certainly be good or bad.

Avoiding these pitfalls can result in a very healthy use of marketing concepts to improve the effectiveness and efficiency of an organization. If marketing techniques are misused, the fault lies with the user.

ORGANIZING FOR MARKETING

When the terms organizing and organization are used, they really refer to two different concepts. Organizing is a process that involves a series of steps that lead to an end product — the organization. The organization, then, is the result of the organizing process. The organizing process is not a one-time effort to develop an organization, but a continuous process which changes as the operating environment changes. The organization can be thought of as a snapshot of the church/ministry's administrative managerial structure at a given time, whereas the organizing process can be thought of as a film of the changes taking place over time.

Organizing for marketing refers to the process of developing a structure to accommodate and assign responsibility for the marketing activity.

Organizing may be defined simply as the process of:

1. Determining what must be done if a given set of objectives is to be achieved.
2. Dividing the necessary activities into segments small enough so that each can be performed by one person.
3. Providing means of coordination to ensure that there is no wasted effort and that the members of the organization do not get in each other's way.

This process should produce a structure of task and authority relationships that enhances the organization's ability to accomplish stated objectives. The end result of the process is usually represented by an organizational chart which shows individuals' positions and formal relationships of authority. When detailed job descriptions, specifying duties and responsibilities, are prepared for each position the foundations for the administrative system have been laid. If current job descriptions do not state that developing marketing plans is a responsibility of some specific administrator, the job description should be rewritten to state his/her responsibility in that task. This, of course, does not mean that the administrator would individually carry out all the activities necessary to develop a plan, but only that s/he is responsible for seeing that one is prepared or providing input for it.

ORGANIZATIONAL STRUCTURES

The organizational structure is simply the relationship of activities, authority and responsibility at a given time within the organization. The nature of the organization greatly influences not only who will be responsible for marketing, but also how much assistance the individual can expect from others in the organization.

Two basic types of organizational structures are the line organization and the line and staff organization. The distinctions between the two are the separation of planning and operating tasks in the staff and line organization. The line organization is the simplest form and will be described first.

In a line organization, authority flows directly from the chief administrator to the first subordinate, then to the second, and so forth. Few, if any, specialists are present in the organization, and planning and operating activities are usually performed by the same individual. In fact, the chief administrator may do all the planning for all areas and maintain primary authority and responsibility for all areas. This type of organizational structure is depicted in Exhibit 1-4.

In the marketing line organization, the marketing administrators are responsible for planning and for the operations in marketing. The two people reporting to the chief marketing administrator are responsible for the activities indicated by their titles. No staff personnel are available to provide support to these marketing administrators. Although this type of organization may be successful for small organizations, its usefulness in larger, more complex situations is limited. To be effective, there must be a division of effort and this is exactly what staff positions provide. Staff personnel are added to help the line personnel perform the various functions carried on in an organization, especially the planning function. A marketing administrator in a line organization must not only develop plans but also carry them out. This means there is less time available for planning, because the administrator is involved in operative tasks of the organization. It is still possible for good planning procedures to be used under these conditions, especially if there are only a few programs and/or constituent groups. However, the analysis done as a part of the planning process usually will not be as thorough, simply because of less time and fewer resources available to the administrator.

The line and staff organization, depicted in Exhibit 1-5, shows the addition of staff specialists to the organization. This permits

EXHIBIT 1-4. A Line Organization

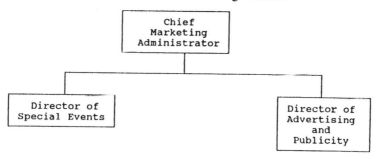

EXHIBIT 1-5. A Line and Staff Organization

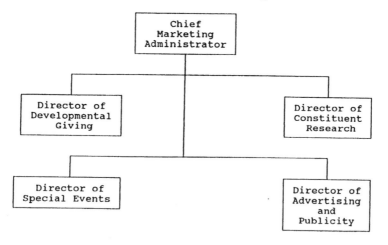

separation of planning and operating activities, which in turn means more time and resources available for marketing planning. The result should be more thorough plans.

The structure in Exhibit 1-5 has added one staff position for research and one for developmental giving. These staff specialists are available to undertake efforts in their areas of specialization. Of course, there are many other ways to specialize staff personnel — programs, constituent types, and so on. A wide variety of potential organizational structures can be adapted to a specific organization's needs.

THE USE OF FACILITATING MARKETING ORGANIZATIONS

The last decision area has to do with the use of the services of facilitating marketing organizations. Facilitating organizations aid a church or ministry by providing expertise in some area of marketing for the organization. The organization's administrators must decide whether to hire expertise from the outside or provide for this service internally.

For example, the organization may conduct its own marketing research survey or hire a marketing research firm. It may design its own advertisements or use the services of an advertising agency. The organization must consider the quality, cost and personnel problems of providing its own service versus using the services of an outside organization. Usually, an organization can perform its own services for lower cost but with lower quality.

PLAN OF THE BOOK

One of our major objectives in writing this book was to develop a tool that will help you in applying marketing concepts to your organization. To accomplish this task, we have provided a worksheet at the end of each of the remaining chapters in the book. After you have read the material in the chapter and feel you have a grasp of the basic concepts discussed, we encourage you to fill out the worksheets with a specific program or project in mind. This will help you apply the concepts within the framework of the specifics of your marketing efforts.

Your attempt to apply these concepts will help you in understanding the concepts and how they can be used in your church or ministry. When you write specific objectives for specific programs that will use specific communication messages and media, you will see how these elements fit together and how your marketing efforts can be targeted and coordinated. A second benefit will be the actual development of a marketing plan for a program or project you need to market.

When all the worksheets are completed, you will have a rough draft of a marketing plan. This rough draft can be revised and shared with others for feedback and improvement. Your written document can serve as a tool to communicate to others in your organization about marketing activities you are proposing. This plan can also be a tool used to get monies budgeted for underwriting marketing activities needed by your organization.

REFERENCE NOTES

1. McDaniel, Stephen. "The Use of Marketing Techniques by Churches: A National Survey," *Review of Religious Research*, Vol. 31, No. 2, December 1989, pp. 175-182.

2. This chapter draws heavily on the pioneering work of Philip Kotler. His book, *Marketing for Nonprofit Organizations*, Prentice-Hall, Inc., Englewood Cliffs, NJ, 1975, is the classic work in applying marketing to nonprofit organizations.

Chapter 2

Getting Needed Information

Marketing in Action

Information obtained by marketing research is invaluable in providing direction or to fine-tune a church and its offerings to the people. Using information provided by a survey — along with wise leadership and diligent work — will enable church leaders to develop a growth and ministry plan for the future. When used properly, marketing research allows the efforts of the church to be more focused and productive.

Marketing research was helpful to a Presbyterian church in the San Diego area. The church had just been formed and was in the process of deciding on a name that would appeal to people in the area. The church had seven possible name choices and church leaders were seriously considering all seven names. The church decided to allow a marketing research study to point them in the right direction. The research team tested the seven names among area residents and uncovered some interesting results. As the names were tested, a clear favorite became apparent. One name was disliked because those surveyed said it sounded like a cult, another was rejected because residents thought the name belonged to a Catholic church. At the conclusion of the study, one name was the clear choice. The survey also gathered information to determine what the community wanted in a church. Church leaders used the findings of the study, along with leadership and hard work, to successfully increase Sunday attendance over a three-year period from 60 to about 800.[1]

THE MARKETING DECISION ENVIRONMENT

Marketing decisions in contemporary organizations are some of the most important decisions made by administrators. The importance of these decisions has also increased the importance of the intelligence function within organizations. Marketing research is the specific function relied on to provide information on which to base marketing decisions.

While the material discussed in this chapter is a little technical, a thorough understanding of how information is used in making decisions and how it should be obtained is essential. Information provides the solid base from which decisions are made.

Most organizations can get help from local colleges and universities in doing research. There are usually classes that involve student projects and professors who may donate their time. Another source of help is from congregation members who may have expertise in working on projects or have contacts with others who can help.

MARKETING RESEARCH

Research is defined as an organized, formal inquiry into an area to obtain information. When the adjective *marketing* is added to *research*, the context of the area of inquiry is defined. *Marketing research*, then, refers to procedures and techniques involved in the design, data collection, analysis and presentation of information used in making marketing decisions. More succinctly, marketing research produces the information administrators need to make marketing decisions.

Although many of the procedures used to conduct marketing research can also be used on other types of research, marketing decisions require approaches that fit the decision-making environment to which they are being applied. Marketing research can make its greatest contribution to management when the researcher understands the environment, organization, management goals and styles, and decision processes that give rise to the need for information.

MARKETING RESEARCH AND DECISION MAKING

Although the performance of the activities that constitute marketing research requires a variety of research techniques, the focus should be on the decisions to be made and not the techniques used to collect the information. Nothing is more central to understanding the marketing research function and to effectively and efficiently using research in decision making. Any user or provider of marketing research who loses sight of this central focus is likely to end up in one of two awkward and costly positions: (1) failing to collect the information actually needed to make a decision, or (2) collecting information that is not needed in a given decision-making context. The result of the first situation is ineffectiveness—not reaching a desired objective. The result of the second is inefficiency—failing to reach an objective in the least costly manner. The chances of either of these problems occurring are greatly reduced when the decision itself is the focus of the research effort.

To maintain this focal point, one must understand the purpose and role of marketing research in decision making. The basic purpose of marketing research is to reduce uncertainty or error in decision making. The uncertainty of the outcomes surrounding a decision is what makes decision making difficult. If you knew for sure the outcome of choosing one alternative over another, then choosing the right alternative would be simple, given the decision-making criteria. If you knew for sure that alternative A would result in $100,000 in contributions and alternative B would result in $50,000 in contributions and if the decision criterion was to maximize contributions, then the choice of alternative A would be obvious. However, most decisions must be made under conditions of uncertainty—you do not know for sure if alternative A will produce $50,000 more than alternative B. In fact, it may be that neither alternative is effective. The degree of uncertainty surrounding a decision, the importance of the decision, and the amount of uncertainty that can be reduced by information cause it to have value.

Decision making involves choosing among alternative courses of action. As illustrated in Exhibit 2-1, decision making can be viewed

EXHIBIT 2-1. Steps in Decision Making

Step 1	Step 2	Step 3	Step 4
Recognize the Existence of Problems and Opportunities	Define the Exact Nature of Problems and Opportunities	Identify Alternative Courses of Action	Select an Alternative Course of Action

as a four-step process which involves: (1) identifying a problem or opportunity, (2) defining the problem or opportunity, (3) identifying alternative courses of action, and (4) selecting a specific course of action.

Recognizing the Existence of Problems and Opportunities

A problem or opportunity is the focus of management efforts to maintain or restore performance. A problem is anything that stands in the way of achieving an objective. An opportunity is a chance to improve on overall performance.

Administrators need information to help them recognize problems and opportunities. A problem must be recognized before it can be defined and alternatives developed. An example of this type of information is attendance data. If attendance was expected to be 500 people at a specific function and only 250 actually attended, the attendance information would make the administrator aware of the existence of a problem.

Defining the Problem or Opportunity

Once a problem or opportunity has been recognized, it must be defined. Until a clear definition of the problem is established, no alternative courses of action can be considered. The symptoms of the problem are recognized first and there may be several problems that produce the same set of symptoms. This is analogous to someone with a headache (symptom), who may be suffering from a sinus infection, stress, the flu or a host of other illnesses (potential problems). Treating the headache may provide temporary relief, but not dealing with the root problem will ensure its return, perhaps with worsening physical conditions.

The same type of phenomenon occurs in church/ministry settings. A decline in attendance (symptom) may be the result of a decline in overall attendance at all churches, losses to another church, or a myriad of other potential problems. No alternative courses of action should be considered until the actual problem is defined. Information aids the administrator at this stage in the decision-making process by defining the problem.

Identifying Alternatives

The third stage in the decision-making process involves identifying viable alternatives. For some problems, developing alternatives is a natural outcome of defining the problem, especially if that particular problem or opportunity has occurred before. An administrator's past knowledge and experiences are used to develop the alternatives in these situations. However, in other situations a real contribution of research is to inform the decision maker of the options available. A ministry considering introduction of a new program may use constituent information to evaluate different ways in which the new program might be offered. Information from constituents about various needs not being met could open up many new types of programs that could be offered, thus identifying new alternatives.

Selecting an Alternative

The final stage in the decision-making process is the choice among the alternative courses of action available to the decision maker. Information provided by research can aid an administrator at this stage by estimating the effects of the various alternatives. For example, a church considering offering two alternate service formats may use information from a group of active members to decide which one to use.

Information collected through research must be directly related to the decision in order to accomplish the purpose of risk reduction. Thus, the focus of research should be on the decision-making processes in general and, specifically, on the decision to be made in a given situation rather than on the data or the techniques used to collect the data.

CONDUCTING A MARKETING RESEARCH PROJECT

Ensuring that data collected in a research project not only are related to management's information needs, but also fit management's time frame, requires a research approach that is centered on the management problem — the decision to be made. This approach is divided into two phases — the planning phase and the execution phase. The steps in a research project are shown in Exhibit 2-2.

EXHIBIT 2-2. Steps in a Research Project

```
1. Define the management problem

2. State research objectives

3. Develop research methodology
   a. Define information problem—specific information needs
   b. Define population to be studied
   c. Develop sampling technique and determine sample size
   d. Determine how to measure variables or attributes to be
      studied
   e. Determine how to collect data
   f. Determine how to analyze data

4. Collect data
5. Analyze and Interpret Data

6. Present Findings
```

An old work adage states, "Plan your work, work your plan"; this approach should be used in carrying out a research project. A research project does not begin with a questionnaire, a focus-group interview or any other research technique, but with a carefully thought-out plan for the research, including: (1) a statement of the management problem or opportunity, (2) a set of research objectives, and (3) a statement of the research methodology to be used in the project.

The Management Problem

The starting point in a research project should be an attempt by both the user and the provider of information to clearly define the problem. Nowhere in the research process is their mutual understanding and agreement more necessary than at this point. Failure by either party to understand or clearly define the major issue will surely lead to disappointment and wasted effort. Many information users, especially the uninitiated, have been "burnt," never to be "burnt" again, by someone who has collected some data, collected their money, and left them with a lot of "useful" information.

One administrator recently related such a story. He had heard a lot about marketing and the need to have information about constituents, although he was really unclear about both concepts. He was approached by someone who offered to supply a lot of "useful marketing information'' for a reasonable fee. Several months after he had received the final report and paid the fee, he realized that he had no idea how to use the information or if it was what he really needed.

This type of problem can be avoided, or at least minimized, through user-provider interaction, analysis and discussion of the key administrative issues involved in the situation. The information provider's task is to convert the administrator's statement of symptoms into a list of likely problems and decision issues and then, finally, information issues. Two key questions must always be asked at this stage: (1) What information does the decision maker feel is needed to make a specific decision? and (2) How will the information be used to make the decision? Asking these questions will cause the information user to begin thinking about the information needed rather than the decision itself and specifically about how the information will be used.

An example of this interaction process will help clarify this point. An associate pastor for a large church wanted some information on the adult Sunday School class members' attitudes toward how class time was divided during the Sunday School hour. The author posed the question about how the information was going to be used in the decision-making process. The pastor then realized that each class's autonomy would not permit a common format for the classes, even if information were available indicating that a different format would be more acceptable to some class members. He then concluded that he didn't need the information! The information could have been obtained easily through a survey, but he would have been unable to act on it. The pastor realized that he needed to work on the amount of autonomy given each class and that any information that would be needed would be used to evaluate that particular subject.

Clearly defining the real issues must be foremost in the researcher's thinking. Information, regardless of quality or quantity, collected for the wrong problem or unrelated to the right decision, represents wasted resources and may even be misleading.

If the problem cannot be defined based on current information, an entire study may be necessary just to clearly identify the problem. This type of research is to identify the variables in a given decision-making situation and to develop a clear definition of the problem or opportunity facing the organization.

Research Objectives

There is a logical flow from the statement of the problem to the identification of specific objectives to be accomplished in the research project. The objectives represent a decomposition of the problem into a series of statements that constitute the end results sought through the research project. The objectives should be stated so that their accomplishment will provide the information necessary to solve the problem. The objectives serve to guide the research results by providing the direction and scope of a given project and they are the basis for developing the project's methodology.

Objectives are another area in which the user and provider should interact so that the research will produce results that both the user and provider are anticipating. The information provider's role is usually to interpret needs and develop a list of objectives that serve as a basis of negotiation for final research objectives.

Research Methodology

After the management problem has been defined and research objectives agreed upon by both user and provider, the next step in the research process is to develop a research methodology that will accomplish the objectives and provide the information needed to solve the management problem. The specific decisions made on methodology are discussed below.

Defining Information Needs

The first step in developing the research methodology is to identify the specific types of information needed to accomplish the research objectives. While this might appear to be an inherent part of the process of developing the objectives, it is usually wise to approach this in a more formal way by identifying specific information types. For example, let us say a research objective was stated as follows: Identify the characteristics of heavy donors, light donors and nondonors to the organization. The word "characteristic" can take on a wide variety of definitions – socioeconomic, psychological, behavioral and physical. What specific types of information are needed in this particular research project? Answering this question forces the researcher to evaluate information sought with objectives and the management problem in mind.

This step could be completed under the measurement area — deciding what is to be measured — and this is acceptable. However, since every aspect of research methodology is directly influenced by the type of information to be collected and analyzed, there are advantages to using this as the initial step in methodology.

Population or Universe

The next step in developing the research methodology is to define the population or universe of the study. The research universe includes all of the people or places that possess some characteristic that management is interested in measuring. The universe must be defined for each research project and this defined universe becomes the group from which a sample is drawn. The list of all universe elements is sometimes referred to as the sampling frame.

It is extremely important that the sampling frame include all members of the population. Failure to meet this requirement can result in bias. If, for example, you were trying to determine the number of families in an area of a town who were unchurched and were going to use the telephone book as your list of families to call, three problems would be encountered. First, not everyone has a telephone; and those who do not tend to be in a low-income bracket. Second, 15 to 20 percent of phone owners have unlisted numbers. Third, new residents would not be listed. The difference between your list (telephone book) and area residents could be substantial and could bias the results.

Sampling Technique and Sample Size

Two separate decisions are called for in this step. The first is to determine how specific sample elements will be drawn from the population. The approach selected depends on the nature of the problem and the nature of the population under study. For probability sample designs, the objective is to draw a sample that is both representative and useful. For nonprobability designs, the objective is to select a useful sample even though it may not be representative of the population. The sample design influences the applicability of various types of analysis; some types of analysis are directly dependent upon how sample elements are drawn.

Sample size represents the other side of the decision. Determining how many sample elements are needed to accomplish the research objectives requires both analysis and judgment. Such things as costs, response rate and homogeneity of sample elements must be considered when deciding on sample size. In some studies, the cost may dictate the sample size.

Measurement Decisions

Another tough question is "How will we measure what we need to measure?" The answer is one of the most difficult ones facing the researcher. The researcher must often rely on what has been used in past studies and on his or her own judgment to decide upon the appropriate technique.

It is extremely important for the researcher to develop operational definitions of the concepts to be measured; these definitions must be stated explicitly. Even seemingly simple concepts, such as awareness, can be defined in several ways, with each definition having different meaning and relative importance. For 60 percent of the respondents to say they have heard of your church is not the same as 60 percent saying that your church is what comes to mind when they think of a church. Yet both of these approaches measure awareness.

Once the planning stages are complete, the written results of the plan should be embodied in a document called a research proposal. A proposal should be prepared whether the project is done in-house or by an outside organization because it is the basis for allocating funds internally and for an agreement when an outside research group is involved. If an outside firm is used, its staff normally prepares the proposal based on interaction with the information users and those with authority to expend funds for outside research.

Data Collection

The next decision area is how to collect the data. The first choice is between observation and interrogation and the second choice is which specific observation or interrogation technique to use. These decisions, in turn, depend on what information is needed, from which sample elements, in what time frame and at what level of cost.

Data collection can be the single most costly element in a project or it can be of low relative cost, depending on the nature of the project. However, data collection is always an important determinant of research value because it influences the validity of the results obtained. Using untrained interviewers to collect data, for example, can produce not only invalid data, but also data that can mislead administrators into making a wrong decision. Careful control of data collection is essential to effective research. Two sample questionnaires are shown in Appendix A. They are examples of the types of questions that can be used in questionnaires.

Data Analysis

One final research methodology decision area concerns the methods used to analyze the data. The major criterion here is the nature of the data to be analyzed. The purpose of the analysis is to obtain meaning from the raw data that have been collected.

For many researchers, the area of data analysis can be the most troublesome. Choosing the appropriate technique and carrying out the calculations, or reading them from a computer printout, is the difference between the seasoned researcher and the novice in many situations. Failure to use the appropriate techniques can result in not getting enough out of the available data or trying to go beyond the data limits in the analysis.

Collecting, Analyzing, Interpreting and Presenting Results

Once the above steps have been completed, the planning stages of the research project have been carried out and you are now ready for the execution stages. The execution stages involve carrying out the research plan, collecting the data from the population sampled in the ways specified and analyzing the data using the techniques already identified in the research plan. If the research plan or proposal has been well thought out and "debugged" through revisions of objectives and research designs, then the implementation steps will flow more smoothly and may be completed in a few weeks.

Once the data are collected and analyzed, the researcher must interpret the results of the findings in terms of the problem studied. This means determining what the results imply about the solution to the problem and recommending a course of action to solve it. If the purpose of the research project was to determine the feasibility of introducing a new program and the results of the research project show that the program will produce an acceptable level of attendance, then the researcher should recommend introduction of the program unless there are known internal or external barriers that cannot be overcome.

This means that the researcher must move beyond the role of the scientist in objectively collecting and analyzing data. Now the role is as a consultant in a framework that states: "Given these facts and this interpretation, I recommend this action." This does not, of course, mean that the action recommended will be pursued by the organization. The researcher usually only makes recommendations. Other administrators have the prerogative of accepting or rejecting the recommendations. However, the researcher must still recommend the action. Failure to do this is analogous to a dog chasing a car—the dog would not know what to do with the car once he caught it.

The researcher should be involved in the problem definition and objective-setting stages in order to be able to recommend courses of action based on interpretation of research findings. To some, this approach may seem to be overstepping the researcher's responsibility to make recommendations, yet most administrators appreciate this approach since it at least represents a starting point in deciding what action should be taken given certain findings. Information has not really served its basic purpose until it is used in decision making.

THE CONTINUING INFORMATION PROCESS

Some organizations have moved beyond thinking of information needs in terms of projects and have focused their attention on creating information systems that provide a continuous flow of information to administrators. While such a focus may shift priorities in terms of the amount spent on information for a data base and that spent for specific projects, it should be pointed out that even if information is collected on a regular basis as a part of the information system, the principles of good marketing research set forth in this chapter are still applicable. The fact that information is collected on a regular basis does not negate the need for relating it to management decisions, for using correct sampling techniques, and so on. The basic principles — directly or indirectly — apply to all information flows. An understanding of these principles will help ensure better quality of information regardless of the nature of the system or procedures used to provide the information.

SUMMARY

This chapter has focused on the purpose, use and overall approaches to gathering information for making marketing decisions. An understanding of the decision-making process, along with knowing how information can aid an administrator, is the basis for planning and implementing research projects. Research projects should be carried out so that this focus of providing problem-solving information is central to the research process. This chapter outlined such an approach. Chapter 3 lays the framework for planning marketing programs.

REFERENCE NOTE

1. Sellers, Ron, "Market Research and the Local Church," *Ministries Today*, September/October, 1988, pp. 58-61.

INFORMATION NEEDS WORKSHEET

This worksheet will aid you in applying the concepts discussed in this chapter to your church ministry.

Answer These Questions First

1.   What kinds of information do you need to make a decision about which course of action to take? Stated another way, if you knew this, would it enable you to make a decision? If yes, is the "this" you specified the information you need?_____
_____
_____
_____

2.   Who is going to be responsible for getting this information? Someone within the organization? An external person or group? _____
_____
_____
_____

3.   If someone within the organization is to collect the data, are there any resource people who could be used to give guidance or input? Who are these people?____
_____
_____
_____

4.   Has a budget been set aside for this research project? If not, where will the funds come from?_____
_____
_____
_____

Now Identify Your Information Needs

1.   Describe in your own words what you think should be accomplished in the project.
A.   _____
B.   _____
C.   _____
D.   _____

2.   How would you recommend getting the data to accomplish the objectives?
A.   What information is needed?_____
_____
_____

B.   From whom should you collect data?_____
_____
_____

C.   From how many people should you collect data?_____
_____
_____

D. What kinds of questions do you need to ask them?_____

_____

_____

E. How will you collect the data? In person? By telephone? Do you need a formal questionnaire?_____

_____

_____

F. How will you combine the data gathered from different individuals so you can summarize their answers?_____

_____

_____

Chapter 3

Planning Marketing Activities

Marketing in Action

To develop a marketing plan for religious programs, it is helpful to follow a basic marketing program development model. One model begins with the consideration of marketing opportunities and a definition of the generic product, followed by a segmentation of the marketing into target markets, and the development, implementation, and control of programs for each target market.

Providing spiritual experiences is the basic product of the religious institution. The first step in the model involves looking at the beliefs and involvement of the church members and congregation, and examining the characteristics of various segments within the congregation and church members. The examination of these segments will isolate various target markets. For each target market that emerges, there is likely to be a unique, "total religious offering," upon which members of that particular segment will place the most value. As various target markets become apparent and their specific preferences are segmented, a program must be developed to cater to the specific desires of the various target markets. Once a program is developed it should be implemented and controlled. With the aid of a marketing plan, religious institutions will be able to efficiently and effectively carry out their missions.[1]

WHAT IS PLANNING?

Anyone studying managerial functions soon learns that although the list of specific functions may vary from author to author, one function common to all lists is planning. Planning may be defined as a managerial activity which involves analyzing the environment, setting objectives, deciding on specific actions needed to reach the objectives, and also providing feedback on results. This process should be distinguished from the plan itself, which is a written document containing the results of the planning process. The plan is a written statement of what is to be done and how it is to be done. Planning is a continuous process which both precedes and follows other functions. Plans are made and executed, and then results are used to make new plans as the process continues.

REASONS FOR PLANNING

Planners cannot control the future, but they should attempt to identify and isolate present actions and their results that can be expected to influence the future. One primary purpose of planning, then, is to see that current programs and findings can be used to increase the chances of achieving future objectives and goals. In other words, to increase the chances for making better decisions today that will affect tomorrow's performance.

Unless planning leads to improved performance, it is not worthwhile. Thus, to have an organization that looks forward to the future and tries to stay alive and prosper in a changing environment, there must be active, vigorous, continuous and creative planning. Otherwise, management will only react to its environment.

There are basically two reasons for planning: (1) protective benefits resulting from reduced chances for error in decision making and (2) positive benefits in the form of increased success in reaching organizational objectives.

Some managers and organizations that plan poorly constantly devote their energies to solving problems that would not have existed, or at least would be much less serious, with planning. Thus they spend their time fighting fires rather than preventing them.

ADVANTAGES OF PLANNING

Planning has many advantages. For example, it helps management to adapt to changing environments, assists in reaching agreements on major issues and helps place responsibility more precisely. It also gives a sense of direction to members of an organization, as well as providing a basis for gaining commitment from employees. The sense of vision that can be provided in a well-written plan also instills a sense of loyalty in organization members.

DISADVANTAGES OF PLANNING

Planning also has several disadvantages. Some of these are that the work involved in planning may exceed its actual contributions, planning tends to delay actions, and it may cause some administrators not to exercise initiative and innovation. Sometimes the best results are obtained by an individual's appraising the situation and tackling each problem as it arises.

Yet, in spite of these and other potential problems, the advantages of planning far outweigh any disadvantages. Planning not only should be done but must be done.

PLANNING'S PLACE IN THE ORGANIZATION

We are now ready to discuss who does the planning in organizations, or the place of planning in the organization. Obviously, all administrators engage in planning to some degree. As a general rule, the larger an organization becomes, the more the primary planning activities become associated with groups of administrators as opposed to individual administrators.

Many larger organizations develop a professional planning staff. Organizations set up a planning staff for one or more of the following reasons:

1. *Planning takes time.* A planning staff can reduce the workload of individual administrators.
2. *Planning takes coordination.* A planning staff can help integrate and coordinate the planning activities of individual administrators.
3. *Planning takes expertise.* A planning staff can bring to a particular problem more tools and techniques than any single individual.
4. *Planning takes objectivity.* A planning staff can take a broader

view than one individual and go beyond projects and particular departments.

A planning staff generally has three basic areas of responsibility. First, it assists top administration in developing goals, policies and strategies for the organization. The planning staff facilitates this process by scanning and monitoring the environment of the organization. A second major responsibility of the planning staff is to coordinate the planning of different levels and units within the organization. Finally, the planning staff acts as an organizational resource for administrators who lack expertise in planning. Administrators who are new to their positions and administrators of relatively new units in the organization may fall in this category.

TYPES OF PLANS

Programs and projects usually require different types of plans. A *program* is a large set of activities involving a whole area of a church or ministry — a youth program in a church, for example. Planning for programs involves:

1. Dividing the total set of activities into meaningful parts.
2. Assigning planning responsibility for each part to appropriate personnel.
3. Assigning target dates for completion of plans.
4. Determining and allocating the resources needed for each part.

A *project* is generally of less scope and complexity. It is also not likely to be repeated on a regular basis. A project may be a part of a broader program or it may be a self-contained event. Even though it is a one-time event, planning is an essential element to accomplishing the objectives of the project and coordinating the activities which make up the event. For example, a youth car wash or a bus trip for elderly church members must be carefully planned in terms of who, where, when, what and how.

PLANNING FOUNDATIONS

Understanding the marketing planning process requires a clear understanding of how a functional plan (marketing) relates to a broader organization plan. Exhibit 3-1 illustrates the interrelations of various planning building blocks.

The foundation for all plans within an organization is the statement of purpose or mission. This is a statement of "reason for being," the accomplishment of which justifies the organization's existence. The second building block is a statement of organizational objectives. Objectives are the end results sought by the organization. Upon this foundation, an organizational plan, sometimes called a master plan, is developed which specifies the deployment of the organization's resources through various strategies. This is a broad-based plan which deals with overall resource allocations needed to accomplish the organization's stated objectives and fulfill its purpose.

Once specific decisions are made relating to the master plan, a marketing plan must be developed for the marketing activities. This is the plan which deals with the programs, access, promotion and contributions which constitute the marketing variables. It is the functional plan for the marketing area.

If there are several programs or services for which plans are developed, then the term marketing program is used to describe the total of all an organization's marketing activities. The combined plans for all programs and services constitute the marketing program.

EXHIBIT 3-1. Planning Foundations

Marketing Plan

Master Plan

Organizational Objectives

Organizational Purpose

Marketing Planning

Nowhere in the organization is planning more needed than in marketing. The complexity of today's environment in terms of social, legal, environmental, economic and resource constraints requires a high degree of skill to provide structure to a course of action that an organization can follow to achieve desired results.

For marketing administrators, the marketing planning process becomes paramount. The marketing concept or philosophy has no impact on an organization's operating procedures unless it is reflected in the performance of the administrative function of planning. The constituents' needs are the focus of an organization's operations under the marketing philosophy, and this is made evident in the planning process. Which constituent segments will the organization try to serve? How will the marketing functions be performed? Who will perform them? What level of contributions will be achieved? These are all questions which are answered by a well-thought-out and well-written marketing plan. In essence, the plan becomes a tool through which the marketing concept is implemented into the decision-making procedures.

An understanding of the marketing planning process is also an invaluable aid in helping administrators organize their thinking about the marketing process and the various methods and procedures used. When they talk about attendance, administrators relate these items to objectives to be accomplished. A study reporting constituent attitudes toward ministry activities becomes another aspect of situation analysis. Administrators begin to think systematically and analytically about the marketing process in their organization, and this in itself may be one of the most crucial contributions of an administrator's involvement.

Before discussing the details of a marketing plan, it is important to specify the relationship between the organizational plan and the marketing plan. The organizational plan is the long-term plan for the entire organization. It deals with the overall objectives of the organization and how it should accomplish these objectives.

The marketing plan, by contrast, is an operating plan which spells out in detail the results of a situation analysis; a set of objectives to be attained at the end of the year; a detailed tactical statement explaining what must be done, when, and how. In other words, the organizational plan deals with what is to be accomplished in the long run while the marketing plan deals with what is to be done in the marketing area in a given time period, usually a year.

The marketing plan does not necessarily differ in format from the organizational plan. In fact, it must cover some of the same basic topics — objectives, strategies, and so forth. The difference is in scope and time frame. The organizational plan is broad in scope and may lay out a strategy which is never departed from if successful. The marketing plan focuses on the tactical marketing decisions needed to carry out the overall plan. The time frame for the marketing plan is usually a year and normally coincides with the organization's fiscal year. The situation analysis deals only with the current operating environment and details only important events that influence changes; the strategy portion contains the detailed tactical decisions which spell out changes in such items as advertising themes, new programs, etc.

The marketing plan is a written document which contains four basic elements: (1) a summary of the situation analysis, including general developments, constituent analysis and opportunity analysis; (2) a set of objectives; (3) a detailed strategy statement of how the marketing variables will be combined to achieve those objectives, as well as the financial impact; and (4) a set of procedures for monitoring and controlling the plan through feedback of results.

The logic of this approach to planning is clear: We must (1) determine where we are now (situation analysis), (2) decide where we want to go (objectives), (3) decide how we are going to get there (strategy), and (4) decide what feedback we need to let us know if we are keeping on course (monitor and control). A complete marketing plan provides the answers to these questions. (The marketing planning process should not be confused with departmental or personnel plans developed under a system such as management by objectives — MBO. Even though the processes used to develop both types of plans are compatible, the MBO plans usually deal with personnel activities rather than marketing activities.)

The feasibility of combining programs or services together for planning purposes depends on the similarities of the needs of constituents and the similarities of the marketing variables required to meet the needs of constituents. This focus puts the constituent at the center of the process and creates a constituent perspective in planning.

One of the most important contributions of this type of planning process is the perspective administrators must take to use it properly. Administrators must study the entire marketing process from the constituents' vantage point, which creates new patterns for administrative development and organization. An understanding of the planning process provides a framework for organized thought patterns for the variety of marketing activities that take place in an organization.

THE MARKETING PLAN FORMAT

An outline of the format for marketing plans is provided in Exhibit 3-2. Subsequent chapters discuss in detail the rationale and procedures used to develop the plan. This book focuses on market-

EXHIBIT 3-2. Outline of a Marketing Plan

```
I.   Situation analysis

     A.  Historical analysis
     B.  Constituent analysis
     C.  Opportunity analysis

II.  Objectives

     A.  Attendance objectives
     B.  Contributions objectives
     C.  Constituent objectives

III. Strategy

     A.  Overall strategy
     B.  Marketing mix variables
     C.  Financial impact statement

IV.  Monitoring and control

     A.  Performance analysis
     B.  Constituent data feedback
```

ing as a process, but develops tools and techniques which can be used in developing a marketing plan.

BUDGETING FOR MARKETING

Marketing efforts require expenditures of funds which need to be budgeted. In other words, an administrator should budget these expenditures to ensure that the financial support needed to undertake marketing activities is available. The three most commonly used methods are: the percentage of contributions approach, the "all you can afford" approach, and the task or objective approach.

Percentage of Contributions Approach

One of the most common budgeting approaches for marketing is to use a percentage of contributions. The budget is determined by applying a fixed percentage to either past or forecasted contributions. The proportion of contributions allocated to marketing may be based upon past results or on management judgments about the future.

This method is widely used for many reasons. Besides being simple to calculate, it is exact and is easy to define by administrators who are used to thinking of costs in percentage terms. Also, it is financially safe, since it ties expenditures directly to contributions.

The major problem with the percentage approach is its inherent fallacy to *view marketing as a result rather than a cause of contributions*. But this method can legitimately be used as a starting point for budgeting and can offer good direction in this process.

"All-You-Can-Afford" Approach

Some organizations set marketing budgets on the basis of available funds. Here the organization spends as much as it can afford without impairing financial stability. Thus, the budget adopted and the monies needed to accomplish the required marketing task may be totally unrelated. On the one hand, the organization could miss opportunities because of underspending, while on the other hand, it could easily spend too much.

The Task or Objective Approach

None of the methods discussed so far is without major fault and none closely approximates a good standard. The task or objective approach — or the *build-up* approach, as it is often called — has the most merit. This method requires that marketing objectives be stated well, and then the expenditures necessary to reach these objectives be determined. The implementation of such a method is somewhat more complex, but the end result is that only what is needed in a given time period is spent. Using this approach, you spend only what is needed to accomplish the stated objectives. This approach requires a great deal of experience in terms of knowing what can be accomplished with a specific level of expenditures.

SUMMARY

The marketing planning process should be intricately tied to the marketing concept. The marketing process described in this text ensures that the marketing concept will be put into the organization's operations through the planning process. The process begins with detailed analysis of constituents and their environments before any attention is devoted to what objectives should be sought or what strategies are needed.

The worksheet provided at the end of this chapter should not be completed until you have completed the rest of the book. Chapters 4-10 discuss the key elements of the marketing plan and will provide you with the background you need to develop an entire plan for your program or project.

REFERENCE NOTE

1. Healy, Denis, and M. Wayne DeLozier. "Developing a Religious Program," *Marketing Management: Strategies And Cases*, M. Wayne DeLozier and Arch Woodside, Charles E. Merrill Company, Columbus, Ohio, 1978, pp. 753-769.

MARKETING PLANNING WORKSHEET

This worksheet will aid you in applying the concepts discussed in this chapter to your church or ministry.

<u>Answer The Questions First</u>

1. Does your organization have a clear definition of purpose or mission? What about objectives? An overall plan?_____

    _____
    _____

2. What type of marketing plan do you need? A program plan or a project plan?

    _____
    _____

3. Have sufficient funds been allocated for the marketing activities you may specify in your plan? If not, how will the money for these activities be acquired?

    _____
    _____
    _____

<u>Now Identify Planning Specifics</u>

1. Name of program or project.

    _____

2. Time period for the plan.

    _____

3. Estimated budget for the plan.

    _____

4. Now, using the outline provided in Exhibit 2-1, write up your marketing plan. Use the plan in the appendix as a model. Remember, your plan should cover all the areas in the outline. The worksheets you filled out at the end of chapter 4-10 should be used as the basis of your plan. These need to be brought together now to form your overall marketing plan.

Chapter 4

Constituent Analysis

Marketing in Action

The First United Methodist Church of Tulsa was considering establishing a Christian school in the new educational unit of the church. A questionnaire was passed out to parents both in Sunday School classes and after worship services. Results indicated general approval and sufficient interest to seriously consider the implementation of the day school. Of the 85 questionnaires returned, 82 were interested in the elementary level. The junior and senior high level indicated less interest — 36 students. Thirteen families indicated that the cost of tuition would be a problem. Seven families stated that transportation would be a problem. Twelve families indicated that their children were too old to participate but were very interested in seeing the school project implemented. Only one individual expressed opposition to the idea.

A school at First United Methodist Church would be a way to offer a quality educational experience. The facility would also be of high quality and would allow ample room for expansion of the program. The school staff would be fully qualified professionals who would be paid as such. "The curriculum would be designed to utilize the finest in solid academic preparation, coupled with an intertwined emphasis on building Christ-like character."

Private education does not have a set price at any one time. The price of private education is determined by the services provided and costs involved in the school. To provide the quality of education that is desired, tuition would have to be set just above other church-run private schools, but below that of a private school that is in its own separate building. The school would compete with the best schools academically, while being significantly lower in tuition. While all these positive attributes were appealing, more careful analysis proved otherwise. When projected enrollment was compared to the cost of providing the quality desired, the school would have operated at a large deficit each year. The project was abandoned.

Nothing is more central to marketing than constituent analysis. This chapter focuses on constituents' needs which are the pivotal point around which objectives and strategies are developed.

The key words in this chapter are constituent and analysis. The objective of the analysis is understanding constituents' needs — which is accomplished through analysis. The word analyze simply means to break into parts. The tools for this type of analysis comprise the primary focus of this chapter.

Once a specific market segment has been identified, its size must be estimated. This estimate becomes a key figure in assessing opportunity or attractiveness of various segments.

CONCEPTS OF CONSTITUENT ANALYSIS

One fundamental concept which underlies a constituent analysis is: what is sometimes referred to as a group or audience for a program or service is actually a composite of smaller groups, each with identifiable characteristics. When we speak of the donors, for example, we are making reference to a large group which is composed of smaller subgroups or segments. This group can be segmented in several ways to identify the various subgroups. The size of donations, for example, could be used to identify at least three subgroups or segments: large, average and small. This process of breaking up a group or audience into smaller parts or segments is usually referred to as market segmentation. The basic premise is that the needs of constituents in one segment are different from those in another segment; therefore different marketing strategies should be used to reach different segments. The results of the analysis should be an understanding of constituents' needs by segment and some insight into the types of strategies needed to meet those needs. This is the basis of the entire planning process if a constituent-oriented approach is to be used in planning.

For each segment that is identified two basic questions must be asked: (1) What are the identifying characteristics of that segment?

and (2) What is its size? Answering the first question helps define constituents' needs and helps develop a profile of constituents for each segment — the qualitative side of the market. The answer to the second question provides information on the size or quantitative side of the market.

BASES FOR MARKET SEGMENTATION

There are several commonly used bases for segmentation. These include geographic, demographic, service usage, benefits sought, and stage in the family life cycle. The section on market grids which follows shows how several of the bases can be combined for analysis.

Geographic and Demographic Segmentation

The most commonly used bases for segmentation use geographic and demographic variables. Geographic segmentation involves the use of geographic areas such as county, state, region and nation as the basis of segmentation. For many ministries this is a logical framework. Many ministries and some large churches concentrate their missionary efforts on only a few countries. They may establish extensive efforts in a few areas and not do anything in others. They are using geographic location to segment the constituents they will serve through missions.

Demographic segmentation uses variables such as sex, age, income and educational level as the basis for segmenting a market. In the market grids in the following section, age and sex are used as two variables to segment the youth market. These variables are appropriate for many types of programs and services — youth, older constituents, etc.

Segmentation by Service Usage

A recent approach to market segmentation concentrates on the usage patterns of constituents. Constituents are classified as users or nonusers, and users are further classified as light, medium and heavy users. In some situations a small percentage of the constituents may account for a majority of the users. Preschool programs, counseling services and home food services for the elderly are examples. Thus, usage rates become important as a basis for segmentation for some programs.

Benefit Segmentation

Another way to segment markets is based on the benefits users expect to receive. Spiritual, social and physical benefits are examples that constituents may expect from a certain program or service. Each of these represents the principal benefits sought by the user; each of these benefit segments, in turn, may be composed of constituents with different demographic characteristics.

Segmentation by Family Life Cycle Stage

The *family life cycle* is the process of family formation and dissolution. Using this concept, the marketer combines the family characteristics of age, marital status, and number and ages of children to develop programs and services aimed at various segments.

A five-stage family life cycle with several subcategories has been proposed. The stages of the family life cycle are shown in Exhibit 4-1.

The characteristics and needs of people in each life cycle stage often vary considerably. Young singles have relatively few financial burdens and are recreation oriented. By contrast, young marrieds with children tend to have low liquid assets and are more likely to watch television than young singles or young marrieds without children. The empty-nest households in the middle-age and older categories are more likely to have more disposable income; more time for recreation, self-education, and travel; and more than one member in the labor force in comparison to their full-nest counterparts with younger children. Similar differences are evident in the other stages of the family life cycle.

Analysis of life cycle stages often gives better results than reliance on single variables such as age. The needs of a 25-year-old bachelor are very different from those of a father the same age. The family of five headed by parents in their 40s is more interested in youth activities than a 40-year-old single person.

EXHIBIT 4-1. Family Life Cycle Stages

1. Young Single (under 35)

2. Young Married without Children (under 35)

3. Other Young (under 35)
   a. Young Divorced without Children
   b. Young Married with Children
   c. Young Divorced with Children

4. Middle-Aged (35-64)

   a. Middle-Aged Married without Children
   b. Middle-Aged Divorced without Children
   c. Middle-Aged Married with Children
   d. Middle-Aged Divorced with Children
   e. Middle-Aged Married without Dependent Children
   f. Middle-Aged Divorced without Dependent Children

5. Older (65 +)

   a. Older Married
   b. Older Unmarried (Divorced, Widowed)

6. Other

   All Adults and Children Not accounted for by Family Life Cycle
   Stages

MARKET GRID ANALYSIS

Marketing planners can use data collected from members, prospective members or viewers/listeners to segment their markets, and then offer programs aimed at specific needs. This is like using a rifle rather than a shotgun to shoot at a target. One develops specific programs and services for specific segments.

One basic tool which can be used to segment a market is a market grid. A market grid is a two-dimensional view of a market which is divided into various segments based on characteristics of potential constituents. Two important concepts in grid analysis are: first, characteristics of potential constituents rather than product characteristics are used to segment the market. This ensures a constituent-oriented view of the market rather than a service-oriented view. Second, characteristics of potential constituents rather than existing ones are used to focus on constituents which the organization may not currently serve.

A series of grids must normally be used to describe a market completely, so the planner must begin with a set of characteristics thought to be useful in differentiating constituents' needs. Each characteristic must be analyzed to determine its probable effect on constituent satisfaction.

Two types of characteristics are useful in the analysis: spiritual and socioeconomic. Some examples of each of these types of characteristics are shown in Exhibit 4-2. Using these characteristics to divide and assign a large group into smaller subgroups enables the planner to isolate the needs of very specific segments and then design programs and services for these segments.

The examples shown are not all-inclusive, of course, but are intended to illustrate the types of characteristics which can be used. A planner must select a specific list of characteristics from the many possible ones by assessing the impact of a constituent characteristic on need satisfaction. Only those characteristics useful in differentiating needs are used in the market grids. A youth-oriented ministry might develop a list which includes spiritual maturity, social interaction skills and degree of peer pressure to segment youth. The primary impact of each characteristic might be assessed as shown in Exhibit 4-3. The spiritual maturity of the youth would certainly influence needs — their ability to understand Biblical concepts, ability to verbalize feelings and desire for spiritual meaning.

GRID CONSTRUCTION

Once a list of potential constituent characteristics has been developed, the next step is actual grid construction. Exhibit 4-4 and 4-5 show two grids. Each section within the grid is actually a market segment for youth services. Notice that as each characteristic is used to identify a specific segment it becomes possible to determine the nature of the services, access and promotion which might be most likely to satisfy needs in each segment.

The two shaded areas in the first grid represent two completely different market segments. Needs of these groups would be different; different marketing strategies must be used to satisfy the constituents in each segment.

In the second grid, it also becomes apparent that the needs of constituents represented by the two shaded areas (segments) would be different. You would not expect a junior high youth and a senior high youth to need the same types of experiences. As a market segment emerges through the analysis, it represents a potential group of constituents with similar characteristics which the planner can select as a target market—that specific segment whose needs the organization will attempt to satisfy. For smaller organizations only one or a few segments may be of interest, whereas a large organization may develop or already have a complete line of programs or services and therefore select several segments as potential target markets. Whether one or many segments are selected, there is a need for this type of analysis.

SEGMENT SIZE

Once segments are identified, the next step is to determine the size of each segment. Most organizations are not large enough to develop programs and services for all segments. For example, a specific church may have several members who need extensive

EXHIBIT 4-2. Constituent Characteristics

Characteristic Type	Characteristics
Socioeconomic	Age Sex Income Education Marital status
Spiritual	Born again/not born again Maturity Level Service Orientation

EXHIBIT 4-3. Constituent Characteristics Implications

Characteristic	Probable Impact on Need
1. Age	Socialization needs, transportation needs, spiritual needs
2. Sex	Counseling needs, topics of interest for Bible study
3. Spiritual Maturity	Leadership roles, Bible study interest

counseling. This would not mean the church should start a formal counseling program. However, if a large number of members expressed this as a need, a formal counseling program would be more appropriate.

The idea of estimating segment size appears so simple as to be obvious. However, many programs and services are started on the basis of the interest of the personnel of an organization in offering the program because they have the needed skills/knowledge rather than the number of constituents who have a specific need. A large church began a "used car ministry" — a program aimed at helping people buy a good used car — because a car dealer was active in the development, only to discover that only a handful of people had any interest in such advice. So what seemed to be a great idea failed because the number of people needing that service was not analyzed.

EXHIBIT 4-4. Market Grid for Youth Services

		Spiritual Maturity		
		Low	Medium	High
Sex	Male	▓▓▓		
	Female			▓▓▓

EXHIBIT 4-5. Market Grid for Youth Services

		Age		
		Pre Junior High	Junior High	High School
Sex	Male		▓▓▓	
	Female			▓▓▓

SUMMARY

An analysis of constitutent segments and their needs is a critical first step in marketing planning for church or ministry. Several bases were discussed by which constitutents may be segmented. Using one or more of these, a market grid is constructed and constituent segment size is determined.

CONSTITUENT ANALYSIS WORKSHEET

This worksheet will aid you in applying the concepts discussed in this chapter to your church or ministry.

Answer These Questions First

1.   Which characteristics would be most useful to analyze your constituents?

    _____

    _____

2.   Do you have any information to help you identify the needs of various groups? What specifically?

    _____

    _____

3.   If you are able to define different groups with different needs, can you offer programs or services to different groups?   In other words, based on resources/personnel, can you do things differently for different groups?

    _____

    _____

Market Segments

1.   For each segment you name below, identify the differences in characteristics for each segment.

Segment Name   Characteristics

A.   _____   A.   _____
                                     _____
                                     _____

B.   _____   B.   _____
                                     _____
                                     _____

C.   _____   C.   _____
                                     _____
                                     _____

2. For each segment identified above, what are the major benefits sought?

<table>
<tr><td colspan="2"><u>Segment Name</u></td><td colspan="2"><u>Benefits Sought</u></td></tr>
<tr><td>A.</td><td>_____</td><td>A.</td><td>_____
_____
_____</td></tr>
<tr><td>B.</td><td>_____</td><td>B.</td><td>_____
_____
_____</td></tr>
<tr><td>C.</td><td>_____</td><td>C.</td><td>_____
_____
_____</td></tr>
</table>

3. For each segment identified above describe the nature of the programs that might best meet their needs.

<table>
<tr><td colspan="2"><u>Segment Name</u></td><td colspan="2"><u>Program Characteristics</u></td></tr>
<tr><td>A.</td><td>_____</td><td>A.</td><td>_____
_____
_____</td></tr>
<tr><td>B.</td><td>_____</td><td>B.</td><td>_____
_____
_____</td></tr>
<tr><td>C.</td><td>_____</td><td>C.</td><td>_____
_____
_____</td></tr>
</table>

Chapter 5

Marketing Objectives

Marketing in Action

Phillip Roark had been the minister at the Bethel Baptist Church for three years. During his first year at the church, he and the Board of Deacons continued operations as they had in the past. By the time Reverend Roark had been at the church for a year contributions had started to decrease and new membership was at an all time low.

Reverend Roark decided that the church needed some specific and precise objectives to develop a strategy for the church. The deacons and Reverend Roark decided on two specific objectives—increase contributions and increase new membership. The objectives were stated in writing in clear and specific terms to ensure correct interpretation and to provide a standard for evaluation.

The two objectives of the Bethel Baptist Church are as follows:

1. Increase annual contributions by $100,000 during the fiscal year.
2. Of the new families that move into the area who were members of a Baptist Church, gain at least 90% of them as transfer of membership during the upcoming fiscal year.

Both of these objectives are stated to occur within a specific time frame and in measurable terms. In addition, they are consistent with the overall objectives and purpose of the organization. Reverend Roark believes that the two new objectives of the church—increasing contributions and church membership—are going to be challenging but attainable.

NATURE AND ROLE OF OBJECTIVES

After completion of the constituent analysis, the next step in the development of a marketing plan is to set objectives. This chapter presents the concepts and illustrations needed to aid you in this difficult task. An example is given of how data from the constituent analysis is used to set objectives. The basis for setting specific objectives is the qualitative and quantitative data gathered from constituent analysis. The objectives, in turn, become the basis for the development of marketing strategy. Realistic objectives cannot be established without consideration of the operating environment and the specific constituent segments to which the marketing effort is to be targeted.

Marketing objectives can be defined as clear, concise written statements outlining what is to be accomplished in key areas in a certain time period, in objectively measurable terms that are consistent with overall organizational objectives. Objectives are the results desired upon completion of the planning period. In the absence of objectives, no sense of direction can be attained in decision making. As one writer states, "If you don't know where you are going, any road will get you there."

In marketing planning, objectives answer one of the basic questions posed in the planning process: Where do we want to go? These objectives become the focal point for strategy decisions.

Another basic purpose served by objectives is in the evaluation of performance. The objectives in the marketing plan become the yardsticks used to evaluate performance. As will be pointed out later, it is impossible to evaluate performance without some standard with which results can be compared. The objectives become the standards for evaluating performance because they are the statement of results desired by the planner.

Objectives have been called "the neglected area of management" because in many situations there is a failure to set objectives, or the objectives which are set forth are unsound and therefore lose much of their effectiveness. In fact, a fairly recent approach to management, called management by objectives (MBO), has emphasized the need for setting objectives as a basic managerial process.

ALTERNATIVES TO MANAGING BY OBJECTIVES

One way to be convinced of the usefulness and power of managing by objectives is to consider some of the alternatives.[1]

1. *Managing by Extrapolation (MBE)* — This approach relies on the principle "If it ain't broke, don't fix it." The basic idea is to keep on doing about the same things in about the same ways because what we're doing (1) works well enough and (2) has gotten us where we are. The basic assumption is that, for whatever reason, "our act is together," so why worry?; the future will take care of itself and things will work out all right.

2. *Managing by Crisis (MBC)* — This approach to administration is based upon the idea that the forte of any really good manager is solving problems. Since there are plenty of crises around — enough to keep everyone occupied — managers ought to focus their time and energy on solving the most pressing problems of today. MBC is essentially reactive rather than proactive and the events that occur dictate management decisions.

3. *Managing by Subjectives (MBS)* — The MBS approach occurs when no organization-wide consensus or clear-cut directives exist on which way to head and what to do. Each manager translates this to mean that you should do your best to accomplish what you think should be done. This is a "do your own thing the best way you know how" approach. This is also referred to as "the mystery approach." Managers are left on their own with no clear direction ever articulated by senior management.

4. *Managing by Hope (MBH)* — In this approach, decisions are predicated on the hope that they will work out and that good times are just around the corner. It is based on the belief that if you try hard enough and long enough, then things are bound to get better. Poor performance is attributed to unexpected events and the fact that decisions always have uncertainties and surprises. Much time, therefore, is spent hoping and wishing things will get better.

All four of these approaches represent "muddling through." Absent is any effort to calculate what effort is needed to influence where an organization is headed and what its activities should be to reach specific objectives. Managing with objectives is much more likely to achieve targeted results and have a sense of direction.

CHARACTERISTICS OF GOOD OBJECTIVES

For marketing objectives to accomplish their purpose of providing direction and a standard for evaluation they must possess certain characteristics. The more of these characteristics possessed by a given objective, the more likely it will achieve its basic purpose. Sound marketing objectives should have the following characteristics:

1. *Objectives should be clear and concise.* There should not be any room for misunderstanding what results are sought in a given objective. The use of long statements with words or phrases which may be defined or interpreted in different ways by different people should be avoided.

2. *Objectives should be in written form.* This helps solve two problems: effective communication and altering unwritten objectives over time. Everyone who has played the game of "gossip" realizes that oral statements can be unintentionally altered as they are communicated. Written statements avoid this problem and permit ease of communication. A second problem with unwritten objectives is that they tend to be altered to fit current circumstances.

3. *Objectives should name specific results in key areas.* The key areas in which objectives are needed will be dealt with later, but usually included in a marketing plan are attendance and contribution objectives. Specific results, such as $100,000 in annual contributions rather than a "high level of contribution" or "an acceptable level of contribution," should be used to avoid doubt about what result is sought.

4. *Objectives should be stated within a specific time period.* There can be intermediate objectives which need to be specified in a different time period because their accomplishment is a prerequisite to other objectives. The time period specified becomes a deadline for producing results and also sets up the final evaluation of the success of a strategy.

5. *Objectives should be stated in measurable terms.* Concepts which defy precise definition and quantification should be avoided. "Goodwill" is an example of a concept that is important, but which in itself is difficult to define and measure. If a planner felt goodwill was a concept which needed to be measured, a substitute measure

or measures would have to be used. An objective related to good-will which would be capable of quantification might be stated as follows: "To have at least 85 percent of our constituents rate our church as the best church in the area in our annual survey." Phrases such as "high attendance" not only are not clear or specific, but also are not statements which can be measured. Does high mean first, second or third in attendance; a specific number; or percent? If the statement is quantified as "Increase attendance by 10 percent by December 1, 1991," it can be objectively measured. The accomplishment or failure of such a stated objective can be readily evaluated.

6. *Objectives must be consistent with overall organizational objectives and purpose.* This idea has been previously stated, but must be continually reemphasized because of the need for organizational unity.

7. *Objectives should be attainable, but of sufficient challenge to stimulate effort.* Two problems can be avoided if this characteristic is achieved. One is the avoidance of frustration produced by objectives which cannot be attained, or which cannot be attained within the specified time period. If an organization already has an unusually large attendance, the desirability and likelihood of substantial increases in attendance are doubtful. The other problem is setting objectives which are so easy to attain that only minimum effort is needed. This results in an unrealistic performance evaluation and does not maximize the contribution of a given marketing plan.

One approach to writing marketing objectives which contain these characteristics is to apply a set of criteria to each statement to increase the probability of good objectives. One such list follows:

1. *Relevance.* Are the objectives related to and supportive of the basic purpose of the organization?
2. *Practicality.* Do the objectives take into consideration obvious constraints?
3. *Challenge.* Do the objectives provide a challenge?
4. *Measurability.* Are the objectives capable of some form of quantification, if only on an order of magnitude basis?
5. *Schedule.* Are the objectives so constituted that they can be

time phased and monitored at interim points to ensure progress toward their attainment?
6. *Balance*. Do the objectives provide for a proportional emphasis on all activities and keep the strengths and weaknesses of the organization in proper balance?

Objectives that meet such criteria are much more likely to serve their intended purpose. The resulting statements can then serve as the directing force in the development of marketing strategy.

Consider the following examples:

Poor: Our objective is to maximize attendance.
Remarks: How much is "maximum"? The statement is not subject to measurement. What criterion or yardstick will be used to determine if and when actual attendance is equal to the maximum? No deadline is specified.
Better: Our attendance target for worship services in 1991 is an average of 1000 per week.

Poor: Our objective is to increase contributions.
Remarks: How much? A one dollar increase will meet that objective but is that really the desired target?
Better: Our objective this calendar year is to increase contributions from $30,000 to $35,000.

Poor: Our objective in 1992 is to boost advertising expenditures by 15 percent.
Remarks: Advertising is an activity, not a result. The advertising objective should be stated in terms of what result the extra advertising is intended to produce.
Better: Our objective is to boost our viewing audience from 8 percent to 10 percent in 1992 with the help of a 15 percent increase in advertising expenditures.

Poor: Our objective is to be the best church in our area.
Remarks: Not specific enough; what measures of "best" are to be used? Attendance? Contributions? New programs **started?** Services offered? Number of converts?
Better: We will strive to become the number one church in the metropolitan area in terms of new converts baptized in 1989.

TYPES OF OBJECTIVES INCLUDED
IN A MARKETING PLAN

Marketing plans for churches/ministries usually contain three types of objectives — attendance (viewing), contributions and constituent objectives. Short-term objectives are stated for the operating period only (normally one year), whereas long-term objectives usually span five to twenty years. Examples of both types will be given in this section.

Attendance Objectives

Attendance objectives relate to an organization's impact on an area and are a basic measure of the level of activity for a program or service. Attendance objectives are closely tied to scheduling of services, budgeting, and so on.

Attendance objectives may be stated numerically or as a percent of the total number. If the objectives are stated in percents, they also need to be converted to numbers for budgeting and estimating the audience size. Examples of attendance objectives are given in Exhibit 5-1. The way objectives are stated must reflect what the organization can realistically expect to attain under a given plan. Also the steps of setting objectives and developing strategy in preparing a marketing plan should be viewed as interactive. In setting objectives, they are first stated in terms of what we want to accomplish, but as we develop the strategy we may discover that we cannot afford what we want. The available resources committed to a given program or service may not be sufficient to achieve a stated objective; if the planning process is resource-controlled, the objectives must be altered. It must be remembered that objectives are not fate, but they are direction. They are not commands, but they become commitments. As a planner, you must not fall into the trap of thinking that once objectives are set they cannot be altered.

EXHIBIT 5-1. Examples of Attendance-Oriented Objectives

1.	Achieve average attendance of 500 for Sunday School by the end of the year.
2.	Have 50% of the potential tv audience view our annual Christmas special by the end of the year.

Each of the objectives in Exhibit 5-1 is clear, concise, quantifiable, and stated within a given time period. Only one of them, Objective 2, requires external data to evaluate whether it was accomplished. Total audience size would be required to compute the percent.

Contribution Objectives

Contributions are a vital part of any church/ministry. While they are never ends by themselves, they are the enabling resources that are needed by an organization.

However, there is a more practical reason for including a specific statement about contributions: It forces the planner to estimate the resources needed to underwrite specific programs and services. A statement of whether resources will be available cannot be made without at least some analysis of the cost of providing services for activities that must break even. For new programs, the expenditures and contributions associated with the program should have been analyzed before introduction. For existing programs, contributions can be analyzed to project continued levels of support. This information, combined with estimates of expenses involved in implementing the marketing strategy, provides a basis for statements of objectives about contributions.

Sample statements are shown in Exhibit 5-2 as illustrations of contribution objectives. Again, nebulous statements such as "acceptable contribution levels" or "reasonable contributions" should be avoided because of the possible variations in definition and the lack of quantifiability. The objective of a percentage increase in contributions is the only one requiring additional information for its

EXHIBIT 5-2. Examples of Contribution Objectives

---

1. Produce net contributions of $180,000 by the end of the year.
2. Generate a 20% increase in contributions by the end of the year.
3. Produce a dollar contribution of $85,000 for the summer youth camp by the end of the year.

---

evaluation. The total previous contribution would be required to determine whether this objective has been reached.

Again, the interactive processes of setting objectives and developing strategies must be used to set objectives that are realistic. The costs of many aspects of strategy cannot be estimated until a written statement of strategy is developed. If the marketing strategy calls for a new brochure, for example, that strategy must be spelled out in detail before production and media costs can be estimated.

Constituent Objectives

Constituent objectives may seem unusual to some, but their inclusion should be obvious. They serve as enabling objectives in attendance and contribution, and also represent specific statements of constituent behaviors and/or attitudes an organization would want consumers to have toward its programs and services. Constituent objectives are especially important in providing direction to the development of the promotional strategy section of the marketing plan. As shown in Exhibit 5-3, they specify desired constituent results in terms of behaviors and attitudes and should have the same characteristics as other objectives. They must be stated in objectively measurable terms and should be evaluated in relation to their accomplishment as a part of the monitoring and control system used in the plan.

Short-Term and Strategic Objectives

The time period covered in operating marketing plans is a year or less, and it is sometimes worthwhile to include statements of strategic objectives in the short-term plan. As was pointed out in Chapter 3, the short-term marketing plan is a part of a strategic plan; there-

EXHIBIT 5-3. Examples of Constituent Objectives

```
1.   Create at least 80% awareness of the existence and
     nature of our new recreational center in the 10-to-22
     age segment of the market by the end of the fifth
     week of operation--October 15.
2.   To have at least 80% of our constituents favorably
     rate our programs in our next survey--August 15.
```

---

fore the objectives of each short-term marketing plan must be consistent with the strategic objectives of the organization. One way to help ensure this congruency is to include statements of strategic objectives in the short-term operating plan. For example, the strategic objective of an organization might be to achieve a 20 percent increase in attendance of a given group of constituents. If its current share is only three percent, the next short-term marketing plan may state a five percent objective, the next an eight percent share, and so on. The accomplishment of the individual objectives, which are short term, can be related to the strategic objective in each plan to help create an awareness of the interrelationship between the two types.

USING ENVIRONMENTAL ANALYSIS DATA
TO SET OBJECTIVES

The objectives of a given plan are based on the data provided in the constituent analysis. In this section, a specific example of this process is illustrated to show how it is accomplished.

A large church in a city of approximately 400,000 had a very low and declining number of youth age 13-18. The church had a youth facility capable of handling up to 300 young people. The environmental factors were, for the most part, favorable, and the total youth population had a healthy growth rate.

The constituent analysis identified three market segments for youth services, one of which was for after-school activities. This was a unique segment with special needs in terms of transportation, types of services and facilities desired, and timing of the events.

The number of youth was found in public records available through the school system, and the number interested in after-school programs was estimated through a telephone survey of a sample of 50 youth. The resulting market potential analysis is shown in Exhibit 5-4.

Objectives derived through such a process represent the realities of the area and also the church's willingness and ability to commit itself to such objectives. This example should also reemphasize the logic in the marketing planning format. The analysis precedes set-

EXHIBIT 5-4. Market Potential for After-School Youth Program

---

1. Number of youth in market area (13-18 years old)
    Total: 37,200

2. Estimated number who say they are interested in
    after-school programs at church
    Total: 300

3. Objective: attract an average of 300 per week within
    3 months.

---

ting objectives, because realistic objectives must be derived from the results of the analysis.

SUMMARY

Setting objectives is the second major part of a marketing plan. The necessity for objectives as well as their characteristics was presented to lay the groundwork for identifying the three basic types of objectives — attendance, contribution and constituent. The statements of objectives given as examples in this chapter possessed the basic characteristics needed to serve both as a source of direction and an evaluation of the strategies developed in the plan.

REFERENCE NOTE

1. This section was adapted from Arthur A. Thompson, Jr. and A. J. Strickland, *Strategy Formulation and Implementation*, 3rd Edition, Business Publications, Inc., Plano, Texas, 1986, p. 52.

MARKETING OBJECTIVES WORKSHEET

This worksheet will aid you in applying the concepts discussed in this chapter to your church or ministry.

Answer These Questions First

1. What do your objectives need to relate to—attendance, contributions, constituents or all three?_____

   _____

2. What needs to happen for your program to be successful? In other words, how many people need to attend/watch, join, contribute, volunteer, etc.

   _____

   _____

3. When do you want this to happen? By what specific date?

   _____

   _____

Now Write Your Objectives

Now use the information in your answers to these three questions to write statements of your objectives.

Objective 1:_____

_____

_____

Objective 2:_____

_____

_____

Objective 3:_____

_____

_____

Now test each statement using the criteria given in this chapter. Is each statement relevant to the basic purpose of your organization? Is each statement practical? Does each statement provide a challenge? Is each statement stated in objectively measurable terms? Do you have a specific date for completion? Does each statement contribute to a balance of activities in line with your church's strengths and weaknesses?

Chapter 6

Program Decisions

Marketing in Action

As Travis Redland, minister of the First Assembly Church, thought about the individuals in his congregation, he realized that they were changing. He noticed two major groups emerging. The first group consisted of single, career-oriented college graduates. In the past, most of the individuals in this age group were married, if not during college then shortly after graduating. The second group consisted of single parents. These parents face an army of demanding new challenges every day.

Redland strongly believed that the church could offer something to both groups. He developed a plan and then addressed the Administrative Board with his idea. For the rapidly growing group of career-oriented singles, Reverend Redland suggested the development of a singles group. The group would be provided with spiritual lessons in addition to a variety of social activities. Reverend Redland told the board he wanted to "bring them in as heels, repair their souls and send them out in pairs."

For the single parents in his congregation, Reverend Redland wanted to provide an atmosphere where parents could come together and share experiences and advice and learn that they are not alone. He even hoped to have activities to which the group could bring their children, such as a picnic.

Reverend Redland told the board that the church must still provide spiritual fellowship through Sunday school and Sunday morning worship; but as the congregation changed, so must the activities offered to ensure that their congregation's needs are being met.

Planning of the marketing mix begins with the programs or services to be offered. Contributions, promotional mixes and access decisions are all related to the "product" or service to be offered to constituents. A marketing view must be taken to understand fully what is meant by the term "program" and to develop programs with the right attributes.

This chapter deals with the concepts and decisions which must be made about new and existing programs. The decision stages in their development, determining appropriate attributes, decisions on the number of programs and various other elements of program management are discussed. These are the major decisions faced by an administrator in developing programs and services for a marketing plan.

Nowhere is the interaction of marketing, contributions and personnel more necessary than in program decisions. All three areas are directly affected, and input from all of them is a prerequisite to successful program planning.

THE NATURE OF MARKETING PROGRAMS

A few examples will help illustrate the broad meaning that the term "program" can have from a constituent or marketing viewpoint. Robert Schuller's Sunday morning program, aired for several years, is called "The Hour of Power." What if the nature of the program remained unchanged but the name were changed to "Hour of Weakness"? Would as many people tune in on Sunday? Would the whole program be viewed from a different perspective? Yet only the name was altered.

A few years ago some Chevrolet engines were put into Pontiacs by mistake. The engines were the same size as the ones that should have had Pontiac stamped on the side. The Pontiacs with the engines stamped Chevrolet did not run any differently than other Pontiacs with the correct engine plates. However, Pontiac owners were so upset that GM had to offer to exchange the engine or give them a rebate. Evidently, the Pontiac owners felt they didn't actually have "real Pontiacs" unless the engine had Pontiac stamped on it, although the plant making the engine may have made all the GM engines of a given size, regardless of what name plate was put on.

A program is more than just the activities that make it up, and a service is more than just its end results. From a marketing perspective, a program or service may be defined as the sum total of all physiological, psychological, esthetic and spiritual satisfactions derived from participation. This means that a program or service must be conceived from a total perspective, and not from a narrowly-defined one of the activities involved. The environment of the program, the name or symbol used, the location and who might attend, are all a part of constituents' perceptions of a program. Not to understand this point can mean not only program failure, but also failure to reinforce several user satisfactions at the same time. For example, a mother enrolling her child in a church's day care program may be primarily interested in a safe, positive environment. But not to consider the choice of the name of the program is to miss a chance to add symbolic satisfaction to the use of the preschool. A name like "Joyful Day Preschool" adds a feeling of a happy atmosphere that could be missed with a name like "First Church Preschool."

For churches and ministries, this is an extremely important concept since most offer many programs. What is a church or ministry? It is really the constituents' perceptions of the whole church or ministry, programs, personnel, layouts, smells, colors, and so on. Again, the total offering must be considered, not just the narrow view of a program in a purely physical or spiritual context.

ORGANIZATION AND PROGRAM LIFE CYCLES

It is important to understand that organizations, programs and specific services go through a predictable cycle. The potential of such a cycle points out the need for continually reviewing what an organization offers its constituents in terms of programs and services. These must be evaluated regularly to determine if new programs and services are needed, or if existing ones should be changed.

The organization or program is founded and grows slowly. This is usually followed by a more rapid period of growth if the organization or program is successful. The growth eventually slows down and the organization or program enters maturity. This is followed by a period of decline as long as the organization or program fails to find a new mission. This life cycle model has been used not only to describe organizations and programs, but also the history of services, ministries and specific activities.

The organization life cycle can be refined for each institutional sector through observing a large number of cases. Dr. John Shope, a church planning consultant, described the "theoretical life cycle of a church" as falling into eight stages:

Stage 1 — The church is organized.

Stage 2 — The nucleus of the church organization survives and grows slowly.

Stage 3 — The growth rate increases due to the confidence of potential members being translated into church participation and membership.

Stage 4 — The membership plateaus. Membership in the church stabilizes and contentment and routine become obvious in the membership and church program.

Stage 5 — Initial decline — membership of the church declines, little is done to reverse the trend.

Stage 6 — Rapid decline — membership decline accelerates, members find logical excuses to join other churches.

Stage 7 — Nothing but a small nucleus of members remains, the church is a financial burden to those who stay.

Stage 8 — Dissolution — the congregation disbands and the church dissolves.[1]

When viewing these institutional life cycles, one must be cautious and recognize possible exceptions. In fact, some institutions enjoy a second life cycle as a result of the coming of a new leader or some other key development. There is nothing inevitable about maturity leading to decline. One of the major contributions of marketing analysis is to identify new opportunities for an organization to return to a period of growth or extended maturity.

NEW PROGRAM DEVELOPMENT DECISIONS

Developing successful new programs is the key to continued progress for most organizations and a key way to avoid decline. Most programs reach a point of saturation, and without new programs or changes in existing programs, they tend to decline over time. Research into program failures and successes and the experiences of many marketing administrators have led to the idea that development of a new program or service should be viewed as a series of stages. The completion of one stage leads to a decision of "go" or "no go" concerning the next stage. Each additional stage undertaken represents more investment in time and money, and it should not be taken unless the outcome of the previous stage has been positive. At any stage, a program or service which fails to measure up to predetermined standards is dropped or altered before moving to the next stage. The six stages in new program development are the following:

1. Idea generation
2. Feasibility analysis
3. Program development
4. Constituent tests
5. Test offering
6. Full-scale program offering.

If the marketing plan calls for new programs or services, these developmental stages should be followed in the order specified whenever possible.

Idea Generation. Ideas for new programs and services come from many sources. Constituents, other ministries, seminars and Christian literature are some of the most common. Some organizations consciously set out to create new ideas, whereas others do not. It usually depends on the perceived importance of new program ideas to an organization's success and the imaginativeness of the administrators. Ideas for new programs must be evaluated by comparing the program or service with constituent needs and resources. This analysis should end with the decision to proceed to the next step, drop the idea or gather more information.

Feasibility Analysis. If the program or service passes the idea stage, the next stage is a feasibility analysis. Feasibility analysis involves answering a series of questions about the new program: (1) What are the anticipated benefits of this program to constituents? (2) How many people are likely to participate? (3) What costs (dollars, time or effort) are associated with the program? and (4) Are resources needed more desperately in another area? Answering these questions provides a preliminary assessment of the viability of the program.

Program Development. Given that these questions about the program or service are answered favorably in the feasibility analysis, the next stage is actual program development. The objective of this stage is to develop the program or service to determine if there are any insurmountable problems and to generate detailed descriptions of the program for further testing. For example, what specific skills are needed to carry out the program? Who within the church/ministry possesses these skills? Detailed descriptions of the who, what, when, where, why and how of the program will result in a detailed outline of the potential program which can be evaluated by others.

Constituent Tests. If the developmental process proceeds to this point, we are ready to bring in constituents in a direct way. Constituent testing can range from a trial program to a roundtable discussion with constituents who are likely to support the program. These tests are especially beneficial because the program can be evaluated by the constituents who will participate in it. This can lead to discovery of both positive and negative elements of the program before it is introduced to an entire group.

Results of these tests may lead to ideas for other new programs, or may necessitate substantial changes to overcome constituent resistance. Remember, it is much easier to correct problems at this stage than after the program is implemented. The rush to get a program started can cost a church dearly when the program fails to live up to expectations. Some ideas take years to develop into successful programs.

Test Offering. After completion of the constituent tests and any alterations in programs or services, the next stage is test offering. In a test offering, the program or service is offered on a limited basis, in a form as close as possible to the final one. This stage offers an answer to a question vital to a program's success: Will constituents participate in the offering in sufficient numbers to justify full-scale program development? This can be considered the acid test for new programs. No matter how well conceived or designed, the final choice is with the constituents. Their votes in participation are the determining factor of success. Unless it is impossible to test-offer the program or service, this stage should not be omitted regardless of how promising the earlier stages have been. Again, the organization has an opportunity to get "up on the learning curve" for the program or service. Given the high failure rate of new programs, it is critical that information from a test offering be available for adjusting the program to increase the chances of success.

In addition to using test offerings to get a more realistic estimate of participation, they can also be used to determine the impact of alternate programs. For example, testing alternate locations can aid in estimating constituent sensitivity to location. Such information is invaluable in determining the best location.

Full-Scale Program Offering. Once the program or service reaches this stage substantial investment has already been made, but the chances for success have been substantially increased. The marketing tasks, however, are still considerable. The decisions at this stage hinge on when to introduce the program or service and what specific strategy to use. The answers to these questions depend on the seasonality of the program, resources and policies, and results of the test offerings.

CHANGING EXISTING PROGRAMS

In many cases, the major decisions revolve around changing existing programs rather than developing totally new ones. Again, the life cycle concept helps in understanding the necessity of changes. Although ideas for changing existing programs can come from any source, two specific sources are constituents and other ministries — and the best source is the constituent. Resistance to participating in existing programs or services should be the focal point of any analysis designed to improve current programs.

Sometimes this concept is so obvious it is overlooked. For years, anyone who was familiar with hydraulic jackhammers could tell you that the noise and vibrations resulting from their use were major problems. Most users require relief after about four hours, even when using earplugs. Only recently has a new type of jackhammer been marketed in Europe which has overcome the problems. Talking with users would have produced the information on problems in five minutes. Just seeing one in use wouldn't require any questions!

Any parent of a nondriving teenager can tell you the problems associated with getting their youth to activities, especially those that start/end at times different from adult activities. Lack of participation can be altered by rescheduling events to coincide with participants' schedules.

Activities of other churches/ministries are a sure signal of needed changes also. The problem is that you are already in an undesirable position when you are reacting to program changes only after others have already changed. However, in most cases, their successful altering and/or repositioning of an existing program or service may be a signal that changes are needed.

The best approach is to continually try to improve your program offerings. It is almost like having a strategy of outdoing yourself. In many churches, this element of responding through changes creates an excitement among members for doing the right things in the right way.

PROGRAM LINE OFFERING

Although many churches and ministries may start out by offering only one basic program or set of programs, most develop a line of programs which may not be complementary, or that even compete with each other. One large church that wanted to orient its members to local missions developed over 20 new programs aimed at community missions. You had to choose which to participate in because they conflicted in days/times offered.

There are a couple of reasons for developing a line of programs rather than concentrating on just one or two; (1) more people can be involved in leadership positions and (2) greater community impact.

Two problems must be dealt with in developing a group of programs — cannibalization and diversification into areas beyond the organizations' abilities. Cannibalization occurs when a new program or service is added and it takes away from an already established program. In some cases this is unavoidable, but cannibalization must be evaluated in estimating participation in a new program.

The other problem occurs when an organization fails to evaluate its ability to handle a new program. Feeding homeless or less fortunate people is a worthwhile cause, but the volunteers and financial resources must be large enough to launch *and* sustain such a program.

PROGRAM NAME

A good program name is not only a necessity for constituent recognition but also a valuable asset. Choosing an appropriate name is an important decision because constituents' satisfaction can be increased, and word of mouth advertising can be used to promote the program.

There are three basic attributes of a good program name: easy to pronounce, easy to recognize and easy to remember. It is important that constituents are able to pronounce the name in only one way to avoid confusion. It is also advantageous for the name to suggest some positive attributes of the program. "Hour of Power," "Praise and Worship," "Joyful Day Preschool," and "Pack the Pew Night" are all suggestive of the attributes of the program or service.

ATMOSPHERE CONSUMPTION DECISIONS

The atmosphere in which constituents "consume" programs and services has a direct influence on their satisfaction with the programs. The lighting, music, temperature, dress and seating arrangement all have a bearing on how people perceive a service or program. Outdoor programs can be extremely successful in creating certain atmospheres, but are not effective for others.

One youth minister was determined to take his youth outside at night during a retreat to a pier on a large pond. This service was to be a climax to a spiritually challenging message. The time was to be a quiet time to reflect on the message. It was a disaster. Frogs croaking, an owl hooting and fish jumping in the water made it impossible to be quiet or think. Imagine all this with 75 teenagers! Luckily, God also has a sense of humor.

The attention to such details can aid in producing an atmosphere that enhances the program. It can accentuate and enhance the impact of the program if properly planned and controlled.

SUMMARY

The programs and services offered by a church/ministry are what produce constituent satisfaction. This strategy element requires careful planning in both developing new programs and altering existing ones. Well-conceived programs and services ease the burden for the other marketing variables. Although a good program alone will not make people beat a path to your door, it may be what brings them back — again and again.

This chapter focused on the decisions related to developing new programs, altering old ones, choosing a name, and the atmosphere of the program. The next chapter discusses decisions which must be made to make programs and services available to constituents.

REFERENCE NOTE

1. Philip Kotler, *Marketing For Nonprofit Organizations*, Second Edition, Prentice-Hall, Inc., Englewood Cliffs, New Jersey, 1982, pp. 81-82.

PROGRAM DECISIONS WORKSHEET

This worksheet will aid you in applying the concepts discussed in this chapter to your church or ministry.

Answer These Questions First

1. Is there any evidence that your existing programs or services need to be changed? (Low attendance, complaints, etc. What evidence do you have?)

   _____

   _____

2. Is this program or service vital to your organization? In other words, do you need to continue this program or service? Why?

   _____

   _____

3. Are there additional programs or services that you need to add to better meet the needs of your constituents? What specifically?

   _____

   _____

Existing Programs

1. Identify the specific programs or services you feel need to be altered. What proposed changes are needed?

Program or Service	Changes Needed
A. _____	_____
B. _____	_____
C. _____	_____

2. Remember, if you can't identify what changes are needed, use the ideas in Chapter 2 and this chapter to generate alternatives.

New Programs

1.   What specific types of new programs do you need to add to better meet the needs of your constituents?

	Program or Service	Description
A.	_____	_____
B.	_____	_____
C.	_____	_____

2.   Now identify the stage of development (idea stage, feasibility stage, etc.) of each new program or service and the action you need to take next to continue developing the program or service.

	Program or Service	Stage of Development	Next Needed Action
A.	_____	_____	_____
B.	_____	_____	_____
C.	_____	_____	_____

Chapter 7

Access Decisions

Marketing in Action

Joe Soloman, the Senior Minister of a United Methodist Church, was facing a relocation decision that would determine if the church would survive or not. The church was founded in 1952 on the southside and adjacant to the downtown area of a midsized southern city. At the time, this area was full of growth and prosperity. Over the years, the church expanded with membership growth coming primarily from the surrounding neighborhood. But in the 1980s the area around the church started to change. Over time the ethnic and socioeconomic makeup of the neighborhood changed dramatically to the point that there was no longer a match between the church and the area in which it was located.

For the past five years, the church noticed a pattern of decline in new members, a drop in financial contributions, and a decrease in attendance. Members retained their membership at the church, but attended services elsewhere. Due to the drop in attendance, the church no longer offered two services each Sunday. Sunday night youth activities were cancelled because parents didn't want their children in the neighborhood at night. During the same five years, approximately 720 families had moved out of the area. Of these, 342 families relocated in a more upscale residential area north of the city. Consequently, the church decided to relocate.

The church commissioned a firm to perform a survey to determine where the church should relocate. The survey reinforced Reverend Soloman's and the Administrative Board's desire to relocate north of the city. According to the survey, in the next 10 to 15 years 6,500 Methodists were expected to reside in the area, proving there was a great need for a Methodist church in this location. This area was anticipated to be the fastest growing area in the city over the next 10 to 15 years.

Two years after the survey, the church purchased 5 acres of land in an attractive high traffic location. They then started to make plans for their new church. As the congregation and individuals in the community started to see the church making specific relocation plans, attendance increased, financial contributions to the building fund increased, and the church started gaining new members.

Four years have passed since the decision to relocate and construction will soon begin on the new church. Plans are already being made as to the programs and services to be held at the new church. The church will go back to offering two services on Sunday, the youth are making plans for activities, and the church is looking forward to their anticipated growth at the new location.

Every church and ministry must make decisions about how best to make its services and programs available to its constituents. In marketing terms, this is referred to as place decisions or distribution decisions. Most organizations face the problem of where they should be located to best serve the diverse groups of constituents that are ministered to through their organization.

The decisions addressed involve the level of service, the number and location of branches or satellite facilities, and the design of facilities. Each of these decision areas is discussed below.

LEVEL OF SERVICE

Each organization must decide on the level of service it intends to provide to constituents. The level of service refers to the availability of the organization's services or programs to its constituents. For example, local church administrators must decide how many times a week to offer services to their congregation. Some members may prefer to have services only once a week, while others want services available daily. An organization which ministers to the poor and needy through preparing meals must decide the schedule of meals. Are they to be offered once, twice or three times daily, or offered on a weekly basis?

Another area involved is personal contacts. Will they be made with every visitor? Most organizations try to qualify prospective members by having visitors fill out some type of visitor card to identify those they want to call on or to allow visitors to request a personal contact.

There are significant personnel and cost implications to these decisions. A higher level of service must be funded at a greater level and requires more personnel to implement. On the other hand, lower levels of service can be offered with fewer personnel and smaller funding. The decision must involve a trade-off between what the organization wants to do and can do, given the funds and personnel available. It is always better to start at a lower level and increase to higher levels. This permits learning how to improve service delivery and also avoids taking away services from constituents due to funding/personnel shortages.

THE NUMBER OF FACILITIES

The organization must decide whether to centralize its services or offer them through many alternate facilities. The most economical decision is to operate a single facility. By having one large facility, duplication of services, staff, and building costs are avoided. Constituents benefit by a higher quality of service, but pay the price of having to travel longer distances.

The costs of operating an organization are usually minimized by a central facility. However, as population shifts and new programs are added, the pressure for satellite facilities increases. Some churches develop a mission church which they staff until the congregation size is large enough to have its own ministerial staff.

Additional facilities must be carefully analyzed because the additional financial needs and staff needs can affect the organization's ability to maintain quality in many separate facilities. However, to effectively minister to diversely scattered groups, satellite facilities or some type of mobile unit must be utilized.

IMPORTANCE OF FACILITIES

One of the most crucial decisions an organization must make is where to locate. In most instances, this decision cannot be altered for many years, so great care must be exercised in choosing a location. For existing organizations the decision is whether to relocate. This section analyzes this important decision area.

One of the serious risks of any location, no matter how carefully researched and selected, is that conditions may change — making a good location a poor one. Population shifts occur, sometimes rather quickly. Sometimes a big new shopping mall can affect traffic patterns and parking facilities. This means that a long-term perspective of a location must be used in the location decision.

Organizations need to reevaluate existing locations periodically to determine whether conditions have changed or are likely to. If changing locations begins to appear as an alternative, the sooner a new location can be identified, the more time there will be to develop an approach to acquiring the land and/or buildings.

CHOOSING A LOCATION

Once the general area has been selected, a major decision facing the organization is the specific place to locate. Even though an area of a city has great potential, if the specific site has inadequate parking or other negative features, then the decision to locate there was a bad one.

The Best Location. Retailers often speak of the "100 percent location." This means the best location for the particular kind of store. This same concept can be used by churches and ministries. This means trying to identify the best location and then several alternatives which can be pursued if the best location cannot be acquired.

Of course, not all organizations can locate in a 100 percent location. There are not many choice locations and not all organizations can afford such locations. A site away from major highways may still be a good location, even though being closer to traffic flows is desirable. Sometimes a tradeoff is involved: farther out from the city but more land for growth and parking.

Accessibility of Site by Transportation. With the maze of streets that characterize most cities, we tend to take transportation facilities for granted. Yet there are great differences, and these can add to or detract from a particular site. In major cities, nearness of public transportation (buses and subways) is important, especially with such constituent groups as the elderly. Traffic congestion and variations during certain periods of the day or week are significant. For example, crowded streets which are made more crowded with factory workers dispersing or with baseball or football crowds can be detrimental to night services or preschool traffic.

The matter of accessibility is rather complex, however. In most larger cities, it is measured in driving time. For example, a location may not be considered if it is over 20 minutes from a major residential area served by a church. This would limit the search for potential sites to those that meet that criterion.

Parking Adequacy. Related to the accessibility of a site is its parking situation. We know that the decline of downtown business is partly due to the scarcity of parking facilities and the expense of such parking. Many large churches have attempted to improve the parking situation by constructing their own garages and ramps, or by arranging for parking at nearby lots. In many downtown areas, it is common to see church signs calling attention to free parking and shuttle service to the church. However, it is difficult to match the parking convenience of the newer suburban locations.

As important as parking is to downtown churches, there are still newly constructed parking facilities which are inadequate. Land is costly and there is a temptation to skimp a little and paint narrower parking stalls so that more cars can be accommodated in the same space. Parking then requires more effort, sides of cars are chipped from doors opening and banging into them, and ease and comfort in parking are still lacking.

Growth Pattern of the Area. Most locations involve long-term commitments. Therefore, location analysis should consider the direction and growth of the area. Are these improving or going downhill? New stores or buildings and modernization efforts are an encouraging sign. On the other hand, a lack of such updating efforts suggests that present facilities are becoming obsolete, with merchants intending to move to the suburbs as their leases expire. New residential construction and new construction permits should be investigated. For larger cities, projected subway routes can provide a long-term indication of the viability of particular sites.

Compatibility of Existing Organizations. Some organizations are compatible with each other — that is, they benefit from being close together. Others are detrimental. While many cities have specific rules for types of businesses which can be located close to a church or ministry, others do not. Night clubs and liquor stores are examples of businesses not compatible with church or ministry facilities.

Possible Negative Factors in a Site. Certain things can be detrimental to a particular site and should be evaluated in making a location decision. Vacant buildings create an atmosphere of neglect and poverty. Poor sidewalks, smoke or unusual noise from nearby factories can be detrimental. Proximity to a tavern or X-rated movie house flaws a site. If the general area is run down or poorly lighted, organizations located there probably will suffer. An even more intangible factor, the *reputation* of a particular neighborhood for crime or vandalism, will be a negative influence.

THE DESIGN OF FACILITIES

Organizations also have to make decisions on the design of their facilities because this can affect constituents' attitudes and behavior. Consider how the "atmosphere" of a church can affect constituents. Many older churches have gothic designs with drab wall colors that may create a "cold, unfriendly" feeling, especially among visitors. Newer facilities can be designed with colors, textures, furnishings and layouts that reinforce positive feelings of warmth, openness, etc.

An organization that is designing a service facility for the first time faces four major design decisions:

1. *What should the building look like on the outside?* The building can look like a Greek temple, a villa, a glass skyscraper or another genre. It can look awe-aspiring, ordinary or intimate.
2. *How should the building be laid out?* The rooms and corridors must be designed to handle capacity crowds so that people do not have to experience congestion.
3. *What should the building feel like on the inside?* Every building conveys a feeling, whether intended or unplanned; awesome and somber, bright and modern or warm and intimate. Each feeling will have a different effect on the visitors and their overall satisfaction with the facility.
4. *What materials would best support the desired feeling of the building?* The feeling of a building is conveyed by color,

brightness, size, shape, volume, pitch, scent, freshness, softness, smoothness and temperature. The planners must choose colors, fabrics and furnishings that create or reinforce the desired feeling.

Each facility will have a look that may add to or detract from constituent satisfaction and staff performance. Since the staff must work in the facility all day long, the facility should be designed to support them in performing their work with ease and cheerfulness. Many of the decisions discussed in this section require outside assistance.

The selection of building color, for example, is a task for the expert designer, not the layman. Color is a highly technical subject, and, when approached from the lay point of view, choice may be influenced by the preferences of the individual. Sometimes those colors that we personally like or feel would be suitable are incompatible with wall texture or atmosphere.

People are known to react significantly to certain colors and their combinations. As a result, appropriately color-coordinated buildings attract better responses than do those with hit-or-miss color schemes. The color of a building or its walls can make people feel that it is weak or strong, dirty or clean, heavy or light, and even masculine or feminine.

Modern buildings use intensive fluorescent illumination ranging upwards from 50 foot-candles. Colors must be designed with lighting in mind. When the same color is viewed under incandescent light, it appears to change.

This discussion should point out the need for the use of assistance in building design, color selection, sound equipment, etc. While this assistance will not come without a price, in the long run it is easier to do things right the first time.

SUMMARY

Every church and ministry must design a marketing mix which provides access to its programs and services. This requires deciding on the level of service, the number and location of facilities and the design of facilities.

Each of these decisions must be evaluated in terms of the funds and personnel requirement that each decision implies. The final outcome of the decision process is usually a compromise between the ideal and what can be realistically funded and staffed in a given time period.

ACCESS DECISION WORKSHEET

This worksheet will aid you in applying the concepts discussed in this chapter to your church or ministry.

Answer These Questions First

1.   What level of quality can be realistically maintained in the programs and services you are offering? Identify the level of quality desired for each program.

      _____

      _____

2.   Do you need additional satellite facilities to effectively meet the needs of your constituents? Do they need to be fixed or mobile?

      _____

      _____

3.   What feelings do you want constituents to have when experiencing (seeing, being inside) your facility?

      _____

      _____

3b.   Are these feelings being attained with the current/proposed facility? Why?

      _____

      _____

4.   What areas do you need the most help in as far as marketing activities are concerned? Are there organizations in your area that could provide the services you need?

      _____

      _____

Identify Needed Changes In Access

1.   What alterations are needed in the level of programs/services you offer?

Program Or Services	Changes Needed
A. _____	_____
B. _____	_____
C. _____	_____

2a.   How many additional locations are needed? Where should they be located?

Facility A _____

_____

Facility B _____

_____

2b.   How will these be funded/staffed?

_____

_____

3.   What changes are needed in design to improve the atmosphere of your facilities?

Appearance Changes _____

_____

Color Changes _____

_____

Sound/Smell Changes _____

_____

Chapter 8

Communications Decisions

Marketing in Action

The "Little Church with a Big Heart" is what many people in Monroe, Louisiana are calling the Monroe Covenant Church. This small church, with only about 100 members, seems to be able to get involved in big projects to help others and motivate others to get involved too. The church's efforts were able to motivate local businessmen to give an estimated $25,000 in equipment and transportation to replace an orphanage's water supply system in Reynosa, Mexico.

When the orphanage director brought some of the children to visit their Louisiana friends, Jim Weathers, a church member, decided this could be an opportunity to let other people in the community know about the needs of the orphanage and the work in Mexico. Jim owns his own advertising firm and used his contacts with area media personnel to ask them to use this as a public interest story. The results were outstanding. The media coverage involved two television stations visiting the church and touring with the orphans, coverage on a morning talk show, plus radio and newspaper coverage. This brought another outpouring of interest in the orphanage and many calls and letters from individuals, civic groups, and businesses who wanted to help the orphanage.

In one year more was donated to the orphanage in money, supplies, clothing, etc., than in the previous three years combined. In addition, Monroe Covenant Church received more publicity than any church in the area. Bob Clanton, the pastor, says people he doesn't know continue to greet him and ask him about the orphanage *and* the church. Bob's comment about the media coverage was a poignant summary of the events: "We had a story to tell and we simply told our story."

NATURE OF COMMUNICATIONS

Communication decisions center on what is to be communicated, to whom, through what methods and media, at what appropriate costs. Promotion of programs, services and activities is necessary to inform, persuade and remind constituents that a program, service or activity exists and that they can benefit from participation. For a market to exist, information must be exchanged. It is information which brings providers and users together at a particular place to engage in an exchange. Communication may be defined as an organization's activities which are designed to inform, persuade or remind constituents about the organization and the services it offers.

Insight into the types of decisions involved in communication can be gained by viewing it as a communication process (see Exhibit 8-1). In the communication process, a source (church or ministry) sends a message by using a certain method or medium. This message is received by a receiver (constituent), and the receiver's words and actions send a message back to the source about what was received and the receiver's willingness to respond to that message. This process is always goal-oriented. The sender is communicating to get a response from the receiver. This response may be holding certain information or attitudes, or it may show itself in behavior — immediate acts or precipitant acts — but a response is desired nonetheless.

The checkered areas in the sender's and receiver's boxes represent common frames of reference. A common frame of reference is a prerequisite to effective communication. Unless there is a common area of understanding between the sender and receiver, no

EXHIBIT 8-1. The Communication Process

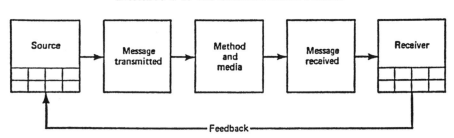

communication takes place. The simplest example is a language barrier. If the message is sent in English and the receiver understands only Spanish, no communication takes place. The symbols (words) used to communicate are not common to the two parties in the process.

One point which must always be in the planner's thinking is that promotion from a planning perspective involves sending the right message to the right audience through the right medium by using the right methods at the right costs. Deciding what is "right" constitutes the marketing planner's work in the communications part of the marketing plan.

TARGET AUDIENCE DECISIONS

There are many potential audiences to target communications efforts toward. When the communication is directed toward members, it is referred to as internal communications. External communications arc used when the effort is directed toward potential members, the public at large or supporters who are not members. Normally, organizations promote to both groups so it is not an either/or decision, but one of relative emphasis.

Different audiences are going to be interested in different information, so great care must be exercised in providing the right information to the right group. If a ministry is undertaking a new mission project, for example, past supporters do not need the same type of information that potential supporters need. The information already held by past supporters is different from that of potential supporters. The frames of reference for the two groups are different. Church members may know what the annual church picnic involves, but visitors don't. Information sent to the two groups should reflect this!

MESSAGE CONTENT DECISIONS

Although the sender is the initiator of the communication process, the process really begins with the receiver — the constituent. This should be obvious, but it is often overlooked in many an organization's desire to tell its "story." Effective communication involves sending the right message, and the right message is the one which will produce the response desired by the organization from the constituent. This is not manipulative, but integrative. The needs and wants of constituents for certain types of information are integrated into the messages that are sent. A simple way to approach this concept is to look at the individual adoption process for new services. This process is made up of the stages a constituent goes through in attending or watching a program or participating in a service. These stages and the questions a constituent wants answered are shown in Exhibit 8-2.

As individual constituents move through these adoption stages in larger numbers, the program begins to move through its life cycle — which brings the need to align the messages with the stages in the life cycle. In the introductory stages, communications messages must inform potential constituents of the offering. In the growth stage, messages must persuade constituents to attend or support a specific service rather than competing services. The maturity stage brings the need for reminding constituents of the services in order to build repeat attendance. Thus, messages must be developed which

EXHIBIT 8-2. Individual Adoption States and Information Needs

Stage In The Adoption Process	Questions To Be Answered
1. Awareness: constitution first learns of church/ministry.	What are you all about? Who attends/watches you?
2. Interest: constituent considers whether to try the service.	Why would anyone attend? What benefits would they get?
3. Evaluation: constituent considers whether to try service.	Why should I attend or watch? Will I get the same benefits?
4. Trial: constituent tries service on a limited basis.	Will the service really deliver the benefits I expect?
5. Adoption: constituent decides to attend/watch on a regular basis.	Did I make the right the right choice?
6. Repeat: constituent will repeat behavior if needs continue to be met.	Should I evaluate other services/churches?

answer constituents' questions and reflect the nature of the service at any given time.

Since different constituents will be at various stages of adoption and levels of knowledge and experience, a multitude of messages conveying different types of information is usually necessary to communicate effectively with different constituents. It should also be emphasized that whereas most constituents are concerned about the benefits received from a service, some constituents are interested in the detailed information which produces the benefits. In attending worship services, for example, many constituents are satisfied to have their questions answered about time and place of the services. However, some may want to know who will speak or sing and what type of presentation will be given — sermon, drama, etc.

The information from the constituent analysis is vital in communications decisions on message content. The needs and motives of consumers become the center of content decisions. Information from testing, where alternate messages are evaluated, and other research to test the message content and probable constituent responses are extremely valuable. If time and money permit, messages should be tested before use and response measures indicative of constituent responses should be evaluated in the decision-making process.

COMMUNICATION METHOD DECISIONS

There are two basic methods an organization can use to promote its programs and services: personal contact and nonpersonal contact. Nonpersonal contact includes advertising, signs, brochures, displays and publicity. Because most organizations use more than one method, they develop a communications mix to provide a complete communications program. The relative emphasis on personal contact or nonpersonal contact is determined by the type of information to be delivered.

Personal contact permits a chance for an exchange of information — a give and take situation. The personal contact allows constituents to ask questions important to them. Although nonpersonal contact may be used to build constituent awareness and provide information on the organization and its services, the complete communications message may need to be delivered by an individual. This is especially true when there are complex questions or special needs of constituents. If an extremely large and diverse group of constituents exists, the importance of nonpersonal communications may increase, but personal contact is still important in many cases. For example, many national television evangelists have area representatives who provide personal contact and counseling.

For other ministries, the major emphasis is on nonpersonal contact because of large geographically-dispersed groups of constituents. Even though the cost of an individual TV program may be $100,000, if five million constituents were reached by the message, the cost per contact would be very low compared to the cost of a personal contact with each constituent. Personal contact may also include telephone calls or responses to letters.

Thus, the mix is determined by the nature of the service and the needs and location of the constituents. Although both methods are needed and used, one is usually emphasized more heavily in one organization than another.

MEDIA DECISIONS

Advertising messages must reach constituents through some medium: pamphlets, radio announcements, newspaper ads, etc. Selecting the most appropriate media is an important decision. Although the details of the specific medium used, messages sent, timing and frequency are usually spelled out in the marketing plan, the planner must also evaluate various alternatives because of the cost involved and the resulting impact on the organization. In many strategies, communications expenditures represent the largest single cost.

There are two broad alternatives in media selection — print media and broadcast media. As with many other decisions in marketing, it is choosing the right mix that is essential rather than choosing one alternative and not the other.

Even within a category — print, for example — there will usually be a mix of various print media rather than just one type. The media types are shown in Exhibit 8-3 along with their relative cost, advantages and disadvantages.

Media selection begins with the characteristics of the constituents

EXHIBIT 8-3. Relative Costs, Advantages, and Disadvantages of Major Kinds of Media

Kinds of media	Typical Cost Range Recent	Advantages	Disadvantages
Newspaper	$5,000-$20,000 one page weekday	Flexible Timely Local market Credible source	May be expensive Short life No "pass-along"
Television	$1,800-$3,500 30-second spot, prime time.	Offers sight, sound and motion Good attention Wide reach	Expensive in total "Clutter" Short exposure Less-selective audience
Direct mail	$35/1,000 names	Selection of audience Flexible Can personalize	Relatively expensive per contact "Junk mail"--hard to retain attention
Radio	$100-$200 for one minute drive time.	Wide reach Segmented audiences Inexpensive	Offers audio only Weak attention Many different rates Short exposure
Magazine	$4,300 for one page, 4-color in <u>Christianity Today</u>.	Very segmented audiences Good reproduction Long life Good "pass-along"	Inflexible Long lead times Credible source
Outdoor	$4,000-$5,000 (painted) for prime billboard 30-60 day showings.	Flexible "Mass market" Repeat exposure	Very short message only

to be reached. Different media have different characteristics; therefore a matching process must take place. The characteristics of the media used must match the needs of the constituents to which the effort is directed. This is done to maximize reach — the number of different people or households exposed to a particular medium at a given time. For television, the audience varies depending on the time of week, the day and the specific types of programs offered.

In addition to reach, the frequency and impact of various media must be analyzed. Frequency refers to the number of times an audience is exposed to a particular message in a given time period; impact is the quality of the exposure in a given medium. The importance of additional exposures to the same message or type of message and the impact of each exposure, together with reach, determines media effectiveness; various media costs determine efficiency. The planner is searching for a media combination that is both effective and efficient.

The kind of analysis shown in Exhibit 8-4 can be used for various media alternatives to develop the best media mix. Although this table compares only radio media, the same approach can be fol-

EXHIBIT 8-4. Media Analysis Worksheet — Radio

	KROC	KLAZ	KJAZ	KOUN
Age	13-25	40+	35-55	18+
Sex	Male (75%)	Female (60%)	Male (75%)	Male (60%)
Education	High School/ College	College	College	College
Location	Metro Area	Metro Area	Metro Area	Metro South
Music Format	Rock	Easy Listening	Jazz	Country
Cost per 1 minute spot 7:30 - 8:00 A.M.	$125	$150	$110	$135
Audience Size	10,000	20,000	9,000	16,000
Cost per Contact	$.0125	$.0075	$.0122	$.0084

lowed for other media. The choice of media would be based on who you want to reach and your budget.

A perfect match is seldom possible, but this approach permits a comparison on the basis of reach, frequency, impact and costs. All these factors together determine the most appropriate medium.

PERSONAL CONTACT DECISIONS

Regardless of the emphasis on personal and nonpersonal contact, every firm has someone who is assigned the responsibility for dealing with constituents. These people are the organization's representatives. Personal contact decisions revolve around five key areas: quality, number, organization, presentation and compensation.

Quality

The quality of the representatives refers to the level of education and experience. The first step in determining the quality needed is to examine the task to be performed by the representatives. If they are basically delivering prepared information, a high level of skill is not necessary. On the other hand, when the information is complex, such as gaining support for a new project, a higher-caliber representative is needed. The quality of the representatives is basically determined by the nature of the tasks to be performed and the importance of the individual representative to the organization. The greater his or her importance to the organization's success, the higher the quality needs to be.

Number

There are two basic ways to determine the number of representatives needed in a given time period. One is a "bottom-up" approach and the other a "top-down." The bottom-up approach begins by identifying the number of constituents to be reached, the amount of time to be spent with each, the number of visits to be made to each constituent per time period and, from this information, the number of constituents each representative can handle. This number is divided into the number of constituents to determine the number of representatives. For example, if each representative should spend an average of one hour with each constituent, visit once a month and average six visits a day, a representative could handle 120 constituents—six calls a day, five days a week, four weeks a month. When the number 120 is divided into the total number of constituents, the number of representatives can be calculated.

The top-down approach begins with the total number of constituents divided into an equal number of territories; it then determines the number of representatives needed to cover these territories. If the total number of constituents were 1000 and territories were designed with 100 constituents in each territory, then 10 representatives would be needed.

A combined approach would consider both the workloads of the representatives in terms of number and type of visits and other duties and the number of constituents in each area. This approach would relate both *constituents' needs and representatives' ability*.

Organization

There are three ways to organize representatives—by services represented, geographical area and constituent type. A fourth possibility would be to combine two or more of these approaches. One of the most commonly used organizational structures is based on geographical areas. This approach is best used when the representative is knowledgeable about all aspects of the organization. This person would answer questions about the organization's services.

Where the complexity of an organization's services and programs does not permit organizing by area, service-based organizational structures are used. In this approach, a separate representative is used to represent different services of an organization. For example, a minister may make contact with new converts, whereas the choir director may call on a family with prospective choir members.

When the needs of constituents are completely different, representatives can be organized by constituent type. A common breakdown used is between members and nonmembers. A variation is key person contact. Certain people, in larger or more complex groups, are designated as key contacts and representatives are assigned to visit them. Ecumenical councils are typically considered key groups and a specific representative may be assigned to this group. Another variation of this structure is to divide by donors and nondonors.

Presentation

The information presented to constituents should not be random thoughts about the organization, but should correctly convey the organization to the individual. Much detailed thought should go into the decisions of the messages delivered to constituents. A well-thought-out presentation of information, ideas and concepts is much more effective in accomplishing the desired results. The presentation of information can be viewed as a series of steps shown in Exhibit 8-5.

Compensation

An organization can compensate its representatives in both financial and nonfinancial ways. Nonfinancial compensation refers to the opportunity to serve and recognition for service. Financial compensation is monetary in nature and the representatives are on the organization's staff. Two plans are commonly used for financial compensation. One plan is to pay representatives a straight salary. In this instance, the organization is paying for a unit of time — week, month, or whatever. This plan is commonly used when the representative performs a variety of tasks. It provides maximum security, but may not offer much incentive for above-average performance unless it is carefully administered.

By contrast, another plan used to compensate representatives is based on units of accomplishment or performance rather than units of time. This plan is commonly used when the representatives are involved in fundraising. It provides maximum stimulus but may not provide much security.

MISCELLANEOUS COMMUNICATIONS METHODS

Other communications activities are often used to coordinate personal contacts and advertising or to increase their effectiveness. They are usually nonrepetitive in nature, but when one type is successful it may be continued for years. A church "roundup" is used

EXHIBIT 8-5. Personal Contact Process

Step 1:   Constituent Identification - The purpose of this step is to identify specifically who will be contacted. Information such as spelling and pronunciation of names, as well as correctness of addresses and telephone numbers, should be verified at this stage.

Step 2:   Preapproach - This step is used to collect information that would be helpful in relating to constituents. Their prior contact with a church or ministry, their personal and family background, their religious experiences, church membership, occupation, etc.

Step 3:   Approach - This step refers to how to begin the conversation with the constituent. Approaches include: (1) Referral, "Mrs. Jones said you were interested in ...", (2) Reminder, "You filled out a card requesting a visit ...", and (3) Question, "Would you be interested in hearing how ...?"

Step 4:   Telling Your Story - The representative tells the story of the church or ministry. It includes information on what the organization is, what it does, and what benefits the constituent would receive from affiliating with the organization. Many organizations have material printed for the representative to give to the constituent. This provides consistency in what information is provided to constituents. It also provides the representative with something specific to say about the organization.

Step 5:   Answering Questions - The communication process must not be one-way. The constituent must be given the opportunity to answer questions and make comments. The questions and comments are feedback that enables the representative to respond to questions the constituent is interested in.

Step 6:   Closing Comments - This step allows the representative the opportunity to make closing statements. These statements may be to set up another visit or to elicit some specific action from the constituent such as visiting the service or making a pledge of support.

Step 7:   Follow-up - The final step is often overlooked by many representatives. A card, letter or telephone call can reap great rewards in terms of stressing interest in the constituent or just letting them know how much you appreciate their time.

by First Methodist Church of Tulsa each year to kick off the new church year. The "roundup" includes western costumes, music, pony rides and games for children, plus a picnic for everyone.

These types of activities can have a significant influence on visitors and members alike. The use of a display which complements and/or reinforces advertising can effectively make the transfer from what is seen in direct mail at home to the display in the church where the activity or service takes place. Examples of miscellaneous communications methods are shown in Exhibit 8-6.

PUBLICITY DECISIONS

Publicity, when properly managed, offers another opportunity to promote an organization's services, but in a way unlike those discussed thus far. Publicity involves mass communication transmitted through the media in editorial space rather than paid space. Any time an organization or its services creates news through the media, the organization is using publicity. Publicity has been called "the velvet hammer" of communications because it can drive home a point in a different manner.

A church or ministry having a well-known personality as a guest,

EXHIBIT 8-6. Miscellaneous Communication Activities

Displays: In-church promotions such as life-size figures, hanging signs or figures, and displays.

Specialty Advertising: Token coins, pencils, book covers, yardsticks, pins, balloons, etc. carrying a church or ministry name and message.

Mission/Service Fairs: Displays set up for a whole group of churches or ministries. A mission fair might feature booths with slides or pictures of mission work. The booths could be manned by church/ministry personnel.

Samples: Samples of music groups, sermon tapes and teaching tapes are often used to introduce constituents to a service or program.

Contests: Churches often sponsor contests to build excitement into a special program. Answers to specific Bible questions may result in special prizes for participants.

Miscellaneous activities: These are the wide variety of promotions used in building openings, church/ministry anniversaries and other special events. They may involve complimentary products—soft drinks, for example—or Bible characters costumed who roam through the audience to entertain children.

starting a new program or moving to a new location are examples of events which are usually newsworthy to the community or audience. When properly publicized, many people can be informed about the organization through the media and the time or space doesn't cost anything.

Publicity can also be negative, since mistakes, fires, thefts, failures, and so on also make the news. Publicity should be managed as a part of the organization's communication efforts.

COMMUNICATION BUDGET DECISIONS

The question of how much to spend on communication of a program or service is one of the most difficult decisions to make. The reason is the difficulty of knowing when you are spending too much or too little. One organization's leader quipped that he knew 50 percent of his communication budget was wasted . . . he just didn't know which half. There are several alternative ways to allocate communication budgets, the most common being (1) a percent of total budget, (2) an amount per project, (3) as much as can be afforded, and (4) the task objective.

The task objective method is a concept needing further explanation. It begins with a complete definition of exactly what is to be accomplished—the objective or task—and then proceeds to determine what must be spent to accomplish that task. When this approach is used two assumptions are made. One is that the amount needed to accomplish a given task or objective can be determined. The second is that the objective or task is important enough to warrant whatever levels of expenditures are necessary to accomplish it. The first assumption is the more difficult to justify, because relationships between communications expenditures and results are hard to validate. Thus, in most cases it is a matter of spending what is thought to be necessary to reach the objective.

SUMMARY

Promotional decisions deal with the communications aspects of the marketing strategy. There are many areas involved, and in most cases a blend or mix of methods, media and techniques is used rather than singular approaches. A communications approach is developed in the marketing plan to communicate the organization's services.

The many variations in communication tools and techniques provide a great deal of latitude for the administrator, and in most cases help is available and advisable from constituents to develop a total communications program.

MARKETING COMMUNICATIONS WORKSHEET

This worksheet will aid you in applying the concepts discussed in this chapter to your church or ministry program. If you have several communications you are working on, you need to repeat this for each separate item, and then lay out an overall plan specifying which is to be done first, second, third, etc., and how much of the budget is allocated to each. This will evaluate your communications program in total rather than just parts of it.

NONPERSONAL CONTACT

Answer These Questions First

1.   What is the targeted group for this specific communication? What are the characteristics of this group that would influence how they perceive messages or where they might receive messages?_____

    _____

2.   What do you want to say to this group? What message(s) do you want to communicate? Are you going to send repeated message to this group about this topic? If so, would a theme help tie messages together?_____

    _____

3.   What media will you use to deliver this message? Are there other media you could use? Have you evaluated these in terms of costs, frequency, reach?_____

    _____

    _____

4.   How much do you plan to spend for this specific communication? What percent of your total budget is required by this specific communications project? Do you have accurate estimates on productions costs, number to be printed, aired, etc?_____

    _____

    _____

5.   What events in your church or ministry are newsworthy and likely to create favorable publicity?_____

    _____

Communications Strategy

First, write a general statement of how communication is to be used in this program to inform, persuade or remind constituents about what your organization is or is planning to do. This is your overall strategy statement. Now use the information from the answers to the above questions to write several statements concerning what is to be communicated to whom, through what media and at what costs. These statements now specify your communications strategy statement.

Overall Strategy Statement._____

_____

_____

Target of Communication._____

_____
_____

Messages To Be Communicated._____

_____
_____

Media To Be Used._____

_____
_____

<u>Budget</u>.   Total _____
    By Media

    1. _____
    2. _____
    3. _____
    4. _____

PERSONAL CONTACT

<u>Answer These Questions First</u>

1. What is the targeted group for personal contact? What are the characteristics of this group which would influence what messages they need? _____

_____

2. What needs to be presented to the individual in this group? What ideas or topics do you need to convey to them? _____

_____

3. Where will these messages be delivered? At their home? Office? Your office? __

_____

4. How much time should you plan to spend with each person contacted? How many contacts can you make each day? _____

_____
_____

<u>Personal Contact Strategy</u>

After answering the questions above, fill out the blanks below to help you prepare for the contact. Remember, if you spend adequate time preparing before the contact, your time will be used more effectively and efficiently.

Specific Person To Be Contacted_____

_____

Day, Place, And Time Of Contact_____

Background Information On The Individual_____

Approach To Be Used_____

Presentation Message (Note: If you have not presented this
before, you should write out or outline your presentation ahead of time.)_____

Followup Needed_____

Publicity

Answer These Questions First

1. Who is to be responsible for publicity in your firm?

2. What types of publicity would best fit your firm?

3. What event/story would be most likely to be of interest to the publics you want to
    reach?

Now Plan Your Publicity Strategy

After answering the above questions, develop a specific publicity plan for an event.

1. Event(s) to be publicized:

2. Specific media to be contacted:

3. Details of the event:

    A. Who   _____
    B. What   _____
    C. When   _____
    D. Where   _____
    E. Why   _____
    F. Budget _____

Special Events

<u>Answer These Questions First</u>

1. Who is to be responsible for your special events promotion activities?

   _____

2. What types of promotion activities would be best to help coordinate your other promotional efforts?

   _____

3. Do you have the policies, procedures, and staff set up to handle the promotions? Do you need an outside organization's help in putting the promotions together?

   _____

   _____

<u>Now Plan Your Special Promotions</u>

After answering the above questions, develop a specific plan for each promotional activity used.

1. Exact nature of the promotion. _____

2. Specific needs of the promotion:

   A. Outside organization(s) needed _____

      _____

   B. Special staff _____

      _____

   C. Duration of the promotion _____

      _____

   D. Budget for the promotion _____

      _____

Chapter 9

Contribution Decisions

Marketing in Action

According to *Giving USA*, the 31st annual report of the American Association of Fund-Raising Council (AAFRC) in New York, 47 cents of every charity dollar went to a church or religious organization in 1985. AAFRC audits the books for nonprofit organizations. According to their calculations, church or religious organizations received a total contribution in 1985 of $37.7 billion.[1]

Religious giving has continued to increase. Many attribute the trend to an increase in personal income of Americans. In 1987, religious organizations received $44.54 billion. This amount increased by 8.24 percent in 1988, with religious organizations receiving $48.21 billion.[2]

The trend of increased giving to churches and charitable organizations is expected to continue. The main factor encouraging this continuance is the Census Bureau data indicating an increase of more than a million people between the ages of 35 and 64 — the prime giving population.[3] As a group, individuals contribute most to charities, followed by bequests, foundations, and corporations.[4]

A major problem for many churches and ministries is attracting a sufficient quantity of contributions to build *and* support the organization over a long period of time. This problem is faced by organizations just starting up, as well as established churches and ministries.

The total amount of charitable money raised by all organizations in 1985 was $79.8 billion. Over 83 percent of all contributions came from individuals, with the remainder coming from bequests, foundations and corporations. About 47 percent of every charity dollar goes to a church or religious organization. About one out of every three dollars was raised by mail or mail-assisted campaigns and the rest by personal contact campaigns.[5]

Fundraising has passed through various stages of evolution — from begging, to collection, to campaigns, to development. Development, whereby the organization systematically builds up different classes of loyal donors who give consistently and receive benefits in the process of giving, is looked on by many as a more long-term approach to attracting funds.

SOURCES OF CONTRIBUTIONS

An organization can tap into a variety of sources for financial support. Some organizations often solicit funds primarily from one source — often wealthy individuals — to meet their financial needs. Kotler suggests that the four major donor markets are: individuals, foundations, corporations and government.[6] Larger organizations solicit from all sources and may make specific administrators responsible for each market. Ultimately, they seek to allocate the fundraising budget in proportion to the giving potential of each donor market. Now let us look at each of these sources. Keep in mind sources you currently use and new ones you could reach.

Individual Givers

Individuals are the major source of all charitable giving, accounting for some 83 percent of the total. Almost everyone in the nation contributes money to one or more organizations each year, the total amount varying with such factors as the giver's income, age, education, sex, ethnic background and other characteristics. More money is contributed by high-income people in their middle years and people of high education. At the same time, giving levels vary substantially within each group. There are some wealthy individuals who give little and some lower income individuals who give a lot. Among wealthy people, for example, physicians tend to give less than lawyers.

Individual givers can be segmented into two broad groups: high-income givers and low-income givers. While the large gifts of individuals often are the primary funds used in building programs, most churches and ministries count on small regular gifts for their operating budgets. The small gifts of $5-20 per month given to ministries usually account for the major portion of their contributions in any given year. Churches count on the regular tithes and offerings of members for their financial base.

Foundations

Currently there are over 26,000 foundations in the United States, all set up to give money to worthwhile causes. They fall into the following groups:

1. *Family foundations:* set up by wealthy individuals to support a limited number of activities of interest to the founders. Decisions tend to be made by family members and/or a board of advisors.
2. *General Christian foundations:* set up to support a wide range of church/mission activities and usually run by a permanent staff.
3. *Corporate foundations:* set up by corporations. They are permitted to give away up to five percent of the corporation's adjusted gross income.
4. *Community trusts:* set up in cities or regions. These are usually small foundations whose funds are pooled.

With 26,000 foundations available to choose from, it is important for the fundraiser to know how to locate the few that would be the most likely to support a given project or cause. The Foundation Center, a nonprofit organization with research centers in New York, Washington and Chicago, collects and distributes information on foundations. In addition, many libraries around the country also carry important materials describing foundations. The most important materials are:

1. *The Foundation Grants Index,* which lists the grants that have been given in the past year by foundation, subject, state and other groupings.
2. *The Foundation Directory,* which lists over 2,500 foundations

that either have assets of over $1 million or award grants of more than $500,000 annually.
3. *The Foundation News*, which is published six times a year by the Council on Foundations and describes new foundations, new funding programs and changes in existing foundations.
4. *Fund Raising Management*, which is a periodical publishing articles on fundraising management.

The key problem in dealing with foundations is that of matching. The organization should search for foundations matched to its interests.

After identifying a few foundations whose interests might match your needs, you should try to qualify their level of interest before investing a lot of time in preparing the paperwork required by most foundations. Usually they are willing to respond to a letter of inquiry, phone call or personal visit regarding how interested they are likely to be in a project.

Churches or ministries with schools or community outreach programs are often awarded grants to develop new programs or to buy special equipment. One Christian school administrator was able to get a $50,000 grant from a foundation to buy personal computers for the school. Another ministry was able to get a grant from a relief foundation to purchase a building to feed and house "street people."

Corporations

Business organizations represent another distinct source of funds. Corporations have been especially supportive of youth-oriented activities, and many larger cities have a Christian Business Directory or "yellow pages" which lists businesses owned by Christians.

Corporations can make more different types of gifts than foundations. A business firm may give money, printing, furniture, food products, clothing or other services. An organization may be able to use corporate facilities such as an auditorium or camp facilities for a nominal fee simply by asking.

One youth director had his youth group get sponsors for a jog-a-thon to raise money for a mission trip. He got several local businesses to provide t-shirts and caps free to all runners. He also got the sponsor sheets and brochures printed by a local printer as a donation to the youth group's efforts.

Government

Other sources of funds are government agencies at the federal, state and local levels that are able to make grants to worthwhile causes. For example, a ministry in El Paso, Texas was able to get a grant to build and operate a facility to house and feed illegal immigrants until they could be processed and deported to their home country. While there, of course, they were asked to participate in chapel services and Bible studies given in Spanish. The ministry staff ran the facility and was paid through the grant.

Other government agencies also make grants to support health care as well as university teaching and research. Christian colleges and other ministries can use these grants to carry out specific projects.

MOTIVES FOR GIVING

Why does an individual give to the church or ministry? This is a difficult question to answer objectively, for it is not easy to "know thyself," yet the ultimate worth of any giving is to be found in the motive behind the gift. It would seem that the measure of a man is not so much in what he intends or says, but rather in what he does.

The motives for giving include the following: obligation and fear, legal compulsion, personal glorification and profit, self-interest, a missionary need and love. Of these reasons for giving to religion, one of the older and more interesting reasons is obligation and fear, which includes those who give to try to appease their conscience and assure their salvation. Believing their gifts would help bring salvation to them and their families, land owners in the Middle Ages would endow the Church with property and other wealth. Legal compulsion was also prominent in the Middle Ages, when the Church had governmental power and could require citizens of a community to support the local church.

While personal glorification, prestige, and honor are often the motives behind the gifts, some givers enjoy the distinctiveness of being paid special attention by the church leaders in return for their capacity to give large gifts. Gifts given for self-interest reasons have the same intrinsic motives. However, in giving to receive honor from men, Christ points out that such givers have already received their reward.

Motivation is not easy to define. Someone once said that every man has two reasons for what he does — a good reason and a real reason. In other words, there are two separate motives for giving; one is external, or how others will view you for giving or not giving, and the other is internal: you give or do not give due to the credibility of the work needing funds.

One of the most important and most difficult tasks concerning giving is the separation of false reasons for giving from pure and just reasons for giving. The Bible discusses pure motives versus impure motives in many instances; without fail the Bible mentions only good things about pure motives behind gifts and how these gifts will in turn bless the giver. On the other hand, impure motives do not glorify God but man, and these impure gifts are not recognized by God and do not justify the giver. The motives for giving are obviously the individual giver's concern and each giver should strive to always please God.

People will give to worthwhile causes if they are informed and motivated to give. This usually means they need to know that their gift, even a small one, can be used and they need to be told how it will be used. Most givers also want a simple "thank you" from the organizations they support. This assures them that their gift was received and appreciated.

SUMMARY

As this chapter points out, there are many sources of contributions. Some of these are more appropriate than others for a given organization, but all should be evaluated. The worksheet that follows was developed to bring contribution decisions into a practical approach for your church or ministry.

REFERENCE NOTES

1. Edmondson, Brad. "Who gives to Charity?," *American Demographics*, November 1986, pp. 45-49.

2. Fuchsberg, Gilbert. "Charitable Giving by Americans Topped $100 Billion Last Year, but Donations to Education Fell Slightly," *The Chronicle of Higher Education*, Volume XXXV, June 14, 1989, pp. A29-A31.

3. Fuchsberg, Gilbert. "'It's All Guesswork' Estimates of Giving Will be Adjusted," *The Chronicle of Higher Education*, Volume XXXV, June 14, 1989, pp. A29-A31.

4. Fuchsberg, Gilbert. "Charitable Giving by Americans," *The Chronicle of Higher Education*, Volume XXXV, June 14, 1989, pp. A29-A31.

5. Edmondson, Brad. "Who gives to charity?," *American Demographics*, November 1986, pp. 45-49.

6. Much of this section is based on Philip Kotler, *Marketing For Nonprofit Organizations*, Prentice-Hall, Inc., Englewood Cliffs, NJ, 1975, Chapter 19.

CONTRIBUTIONS WORKSHEET

This worksheet will aid you in applying the concepts discussed in this chapter to your church or ministry. It brings together all the information that has been discussed so far into a concise audience-centered presentation. It is a description of the ministry, its needs, and a specific request put into the potential supporter's language. This is called a case statement. A case statement is always presented in the language of the person or group to whom it is being given. People empathize best when they hear a message they don't have to translate.

Listed below are seven basic questions that should be answered before making a presentation or request for support to any church or ministry. Note that these questions need to be answered in the best possible way to communicate to each potential supporter.

Answer These Questions First

1. What needs exist for your ministry? Briefly describe your mission field, who and where they are.

    _____

    _____

2. Why should the potential supporter support your organization? Are you the only person or agency reaching these people? Do you have particular abilities or experience that will better equip you to serve?

    _____

    _____

3. What do you hope to achieve in your mission? State your greatest ambitions with all the enthusiasm that carries you into the field. People want to know what a typical end product of your work will be.

    _____

    _____

4. What is your total ministry cost? Money is not the only factor here. Lend importance to your decision by stating what the cost will be. Your mission will also need a blanket of prayer from a faithful partner. Let others know specific things you want upheld in prayer.

   _____

   _____

5. How soon do you need to raise all of your support? Give your supporters a target date of short-term and long-term goals, and keep them informed of your progress.

   _____

   _____

6. What are you asking of me? When presenting your case in a letter, this is as far as you should go. Tell the reader you plan to call to get together and discuss how he or she can help.

   _____

   _____

7. What will (or will not) happen if you do not receive support? Usually put in a closing statement; this may lend greater urgency to your plan. For example, plans for church planting in Mexico will be postponed. The point is that something will be held up, changed, or lessened when you do not receive support for your mission.

   _____

   _____

Ideally, this kind of case statement is best suited for a written presentation. The following case statement will be best suited for face-to-face presentation. This need not be fancy, but it should be neat and well copied. We suggest that at least the cover (with the theme statement) should be professionally designed and printed. Each topic listed below should be on a separate, single page. The writing should be brief and the information easily accessible. The following is a suggested outline for producing an effective case:

Now Develop Your Case Statement

1. The Theme: A brief three to five word summary statement that captures the mission idea of the organization. This will be with the title page with the full name of your organization.

     _____

     _____

2. The Mission: What is the general purpose of the organization?

     _____

     _____

3. The Goals: Stated in personal terms, what does the organization want to see happen? Generally, how is the mission going to be accomplished?

     _____

     _____

4. The Program: State the quantifiable objectives for a specific period of time for the ministry. What are the chief programs and classes available?

     _____

     _____

5. The Impact of Accomplishments: Describe how the organization has met its previous goals since its inception.

     _____

     _____

6.   <u>The Vision for the Future</u>: What does the organization specifically plan to accomplish (and how) in the next few years? What measures will be used to gauge the accomplishments?

_____

_____

7.   <u>The Development Plan</u>: Present the total need (personal, organizational, money) of the organization and the time frame the need covers.

_____

_____

8.   <u>Support Opportunities</u>: Divide the total budget into several categories: scholarship fund, building fund and general operations fund. Suggest different ways for people to give.

_____

_____

9.   <u>Organization Profile</u>: List some of the most pertinent characteristics of your organization, the number and location of your staff, etc.

_____

_____

All of this material should be compiled and presented in written form. Other presentation forms, such as slides, can also be used to make a presentation, but you need to make sure there is a written case statement which can be read and evaluated.

Chapter 10

Monitoring and Controlling Marketing Activities

Marketing in Action

Using data to monitor and control marketing plans can be compared to setting out on a journey with a road map. The process includes identifying your destination (objective), determining the best route to your destination (strategy), and then departing for your trip (implementation of your strategy).

During the journey, you look for highway signs (feedback) to tell you if you are on the way to your objective. Signs along the way quickly reveal if you have made a wrong turn, and you can alter your course to get back on the right road. When you reach your destination, a new route (strategy) is needed to get you somewhere else.

Imagine what would happen if there were no road signs during your trip to let you know if you were on the right road. It might be too late to continue the trip by the time you realized you were traveling in the wrong direction. Yet, many churches are involved in a similar situation, failing to analyze results to determine if objectives are being accomplished.

Failure to establish procedures to monitor and control the marketing process can lead to less than optimal performance. A plan is not complete until the controls are identified, and the procedures for recording and transmitting control information to the administrators of the plan are established.

Simple approaches to controlling marketing activities often can produce good results. For example, if your church changed your advertising in the yellow pages from just your church name listing to a display ad that lists Sunday school and worship time, Bible study meetings, location, and telephone number, you may want to check whether this ad is successful. Simply have the person who answers the phone ask how the people wanting information found out about your church. Over a ten- to twelve-month period, you would be able to show the number of calls that could be traced to your ad.[1]

Many organizations fail to understand the importance of establishing procedures to monitor and control the marketing process — a failing that leads to less than optimal performance. This chapter reviews the need for control, what is to be controlled, and some control procedures. Control should be a natural follow-through in developing a plan as discussed in Chapter 3. No plan should be considered complete until controls are identified and the procedures for recording and transmitting control information to administrators are established.

INTEGRATION OF PLANNING AND CONTROL

Planning and control should be integral processes. In fact, planning was defined as a process that included establishing a system for feedback of results. This feedback reflects the organization's performance in reaching its objectives through implementation of the marketing plan. The relationship between planning and control is depicted in Exhibit 10-1.

The planning process results in a specific plan being developed for a program and/or service. This plan is implemented (marketing activities are performed in the manner described in the plan) and results are produced. These results are attendance, contributions, and accompanying constituent attitudes, preferences and behaviors. Information on these results and other related factors is given to administrators, who compare the results with objectives to evaluate performance. This performance evaluation identifies the areas where decisions must be made. The actual decision making controls the plan by altering it to accomplish stated objectives and a new cycle begins. The information flows are the key to a good control system. Deciding what information is provided to which managers in what time periods is the essence of a control system.

EXHIBIT 10-1. Planning and Control Model

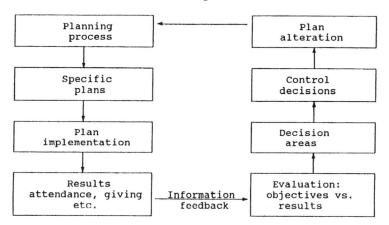

TIMING OF INFORMATION FLOWS

The long-run marketing plan is composed of many short-run plans. An economist once noted that "We plan in the long run but live in the short run." If each of our short-run plans is controlled properly, the long-run plans are more likely to be controlled. The administrator cannot afford to wait for the time period of a plan to pass before control information is available. The information must be available within a time frame which is long enough to allow results to accrue, but short enough to allow actions to align results with objectives. Although some types of organizations may find weekly or bimonthly results necessary, most organizations can adequately control operations with monthly or quarterly reports. Cumulative monthly or quarterly reports become annual reports, which in turn become the feedback needed to control the plan.

PERFORMANCE EVALUATION AND CONTROL

Performance should be evaluated in many areas to provide a complete analysis of what the results are and what caused them. The four key control areas are attendance, promotional activity cost, contributions and constituents' attitudes. Objectives should have been established in all of these areas for the plan.

Attendance Control

Attendance control data are provided from an analysis of attendance for individual programs or services. Attendance can be evaluated on a program-by-program basis by developing a performance report as shown in Exhibit 10-2. When such a format is used, the attendance objectives stated in the plan are broken down on a quarterly basis and become the standard against which actual attendance results are compared. Number and percentage variations are calculated, because in some instances a small percentage can result in a large number variation.

A performance index can be calculated by dividing actual attendance by the attendance objective. Index numbers of about 1.00 indicate that expected and actual performance are about equal. Numbers larger than 1.00 indicate above-expected performance and numbers below 1.00 reveal below-expected performance. Index numbers are especially useful when a large number of programs is involved, because they enable administrators to identify those programs which need immediate attention.

Promotional Activity Control

Promotional activity is another important area necessitating control. It should include assessment of personal and nonpersonal means of contacting constituents.

Personal Contact Data

A great deal of performance analysis can be done on personal contact data. These data can be divided into qualitative and quantitative inputs.

Qualitative inputs:
1. Time management
2. Planning effort
3. Quality of presentation
4. Church/Ministry knowledge
5. Personal appearance and health
6. Personality and attitudes

Quantitative inputs:

1. Days worked
2. Calls per day
3. Proportion of time spent in contacts
4. Expenses
5. Miles traveled per contact

Analysis of these facts will help an administrator evaluate the efficiency of the personal contact effort. For many of these input factors, an average can be computed to serve as a standard for analyzing individual personnel. If the number of contacts per day for one representative is three and the average is six, this case warrants attention. The low calls per day could be caused by a large, sparsely populated territory, or it could be that the person is spending too much time with each constituent. Whatever the problem, management must be alerted to its existence.

Advertising Data

Advertising inputs are difficult to evaluate, but must be dealt with nonetheless. Several factors can be evaluated which help determine the efficiency of this input:

1. Level of advertising
2. Readership/viewing statistics
3. Cost per thousand
4. Number of inquiries stimulated by an ad
5. Number of inquiries that lead to a visit
6. Changes in attendance generated by an ad campaign

EXHIBIT 10-2. Attendance and Performance Report for Quarter 1 (by Program)

Program	Attendance Objective	Actual Attendance	Variation	% Variation	Index Performance
A	1000.	900.	100.	− 10.0	.90
B	950.	1020.	+ 70.	+ 7.4	1.07
C	1200.	920.	− 280.	− 23.0	.77
D	2000.	2030.	+ 30.	+ 1.5	1.02

These measures help evaluate the results of advertising decisions. Tracking these data over several years can help identify successful appeals, ads or media. The key to evaluating performance is the setting of objectives, which become the standards by which actual performance can be evaluated.

Contribution/Cost Controls

Several tools are available for establishing cost control procedures, including budgets, expense ratios and activity costs analysis. Budgets are a common tool used by most organizations for anticipating expense levels on a yearly basis. The budget is often established by using historical percentages of various expenses as a percent of sales. Thus, once the total level of expected contributions is established, expense items can be budgeted as a percent of total sales. If zero-based budgeting is used, the objectives to be accomplished must be specified and the expenditures necessary to accomplish these objectives estimated. The estimates are the budgeted expenses for the time period.

Contributions are controlled by tracing contributions on a weekly or at least a monthly basis. While many organizations have an annual drive for pledges, others are continually seeking contributions from constituents. A prerequisite to controlling contributions is an annual projection of operating expenses. This projection, broken down on a quarterly or monthly basis, becomes the standard from which deviations are analyzed. For example, a church with a projected budget of $500,000 for the next fiscal year would be expecting about $125,000 per quarter, or $41,667 per month. If there were large variations related to certain times of the year, even the variations can be analyzed to determine the proportion of the budgeted amount given per month. If, historically, 20 percent of the budget were given during December, then 20 percent of next year's budget becomes the expected level of contributions to be used as the standard.

The same type of analysis used to control attendance (shown in Exhibit 10-2) can be used to analyze data on contributions. This type of analysis should be performed on a timely basis to enable expansion or cutbacks of programs when contribution levels go above or below the expected amounts for the period.

Once the budget is established, expense variance analysis by line item or expenditure category is used to control costs. Although it is not possible to establish standard costs for marketing expenditures, the budget amounts are the standards used to perform variance analysis. A typical procedure is to prepare monthly or quarterly budget reports showing the amount budgeted for the time period and the dollar and percentage variation from the budgeted amount, if any exists. Expenditure patterns which vary from the budgeted amounts are then analyzed to determine why the variations occurred.

Expense ratio analysis is another tool used to control costs. An important goal of every plan is to maintain the desired relationship between expenditures and results. Calculations of expense ratios provide information on what this relationship is at any time. Monthly, quarterly and yearly ratio calculations should satisfy most managers' needs for this type of data.

Common ratios are as follows:

1. Administrative expense ratio
2. Personal contacts expense ratio
3. Cost per personal contact
4. Advertising expense ratio

Many other financial ratios, such as percent of pledges given, percent pledging, etc., also provide measures which can be used to reduce or maintain cost levels.

Activity cost analysis is also very useful. This type of analysis permits evaluation of cost by individual activity, such as a fundraising dinner. Analysis of these costs in relation to pledges produced is a key type of analysis for identifying effective and ineffective activities.

Constituent Feedback

The final area of performance evaluation is constituents, and involves analysis of awareness, knowledge, attitudes and behaviors. Chapter 8 pointed out that communications efforts are goal oriented. The goals are to have constituents become aware of programs, services, or personnel; possess certain knowledge; and exhibit certain attitudes and behaviors. If these are specified, as they should be, in the objective statements, these objectives are the standards to which current constituent data are compared.

Data on constituents must be collected on a regular basis. There are many ways to collect data, as pointed out in Chapter 2. Constituent data are especially valuable if collected over a long period of time, because awareness levels, attitudes and behavior can be analyzed to reveal trends and areas for further investigation. Also, changes in the constituents' attributes can be related to marketing activities, such as the introduction of a new promotional theme or program.

ESTABLISHING PROCEDURES

It should be pointed out that none of the performance evaluation data described are going to be available unless they are requested and funds are made available to finance them. Thus, data collecting and reporting procedures must be set up by the administrators who are going to use the control data in decision making.

The procedures will usually change over time as new types of analysis or reporting times are found to be better than others. The most important requirement is that the data meet the needs of administrators in taking corrective actions to control activities.

SUMMARY

No planning process should be considered complete until monitoring and control procedures have been established. Without such information, it is impossible to manage marketing activities with any sense of clarity about what is actually happening in the organization.

Performance evaluation is vital for control decisions. Information tells a manager what has happened, and serves as the basis for any actions needed to control the activities of the organization toward predetermined objectives.

REFERENCE NOTE

1. Adapted from Robert E. Stevens and David Loudon, "Controlling Market Activities," *Law Marketing Exchange*, September 1989, pp. 5-6.

MARKETING CONTROL WORKSHEET

This worksheet will aid you in applying the concepts discussed in this chapter to your church or ministry.

<u>Answer The Following Questions</u>

1. What kinds of information do you need to evaluate a program's or service's success?_____

_____

_____

2. Who should receive and review this information?

_____

_____

_____

3. What time periods do you want to use to analyze the data? Weekly? Monthly?

_____

_____

_____

4. What record keeping system do you need to devise to make sure the information you want is recorded for the time periods you specified in question 3?_____

_____

_____

NOW SET UP YOUR CONTROL PROCEDURES

1. Specify the areas to be controlled:

   A. _____

   B. _____

C. _____

D. _____

2. Specify the format of the data for each area. (Is it to be numbers by month by program? Do you want number and percentage variations?)

    A. _____

    B. _____

    C. _____

    D. _____

3. Specify how the data are to be collected, who is to collect and analyze the data, and who is to receive the results of the analysis:

    A. How will the data is to be collected?_____

    _____

    B. Who has responsibility to collect and analyze the data?

    _____

    _____

    C. Who is to receive which type of analysis?

    Administrator/Pastor   Types of Analysis

    1._____   1._____

    2._____   2._____

    3._____   3._____

    4._____   4._____

Appendix A:
Sample Church/Ministry
Questionnaires

ADULT SUNDAY SCHOOL SURVEY

<u>FIRST, PLEASE ANSWER THESE QUESTIONS THAT PERTAIN TO THE CLASS YOU
BELONG TO</u>.

1. What class are you a member of?
   _____ Saints and Sinners   _____ Fellowship Class
   _____ Joynor Class   _____ Seekers Class
   _____ Beacon Class   _____ Asbury Class
   _____ Circle Class   _____ New Covenant
   _____ Builders Class

2. What is the approximate size of the class?
   _____ 10   _____ 10-15   _____ 15-20   _____ 20-25   _____ 25

3. The class would be most effective if it were:
   _____ larger   _____ the same size   _____ smaller

4. How often do you attend your sunday school class?
   _____ 1 time a mo.   _____ 2 times a mo.   _____ 3 times a mo.
   _____ every week

5. In a typical month, how many times would your class meet other than
   in church?
   _____ none   _____ 1 time   _____ 2 times   _____ 3 times   _____ 4 times
   _____ 5 times

6. The length of the terms for officers should:
   _____ be increased   _____ stay the same   _____ be decreased

7 I feel comfortable (accepted) in the class.

   (agree)   1   2   3   4   5   6   7   (disagree)

8. The class is very organized.

   (agree)   1   2   3   4   5   6   7   (disagree)

9. Too much time is spent on "class business."

   (agree)   1   2   3   4   5   6   7   (disagree)

THE NEXT QUESTIONS EVALUATE ALL THE CLASSES WHICH ARE OFFERED AND THEIR
TEACHERS.

PLEASE EVALUATE EACH CLASS YOU HAVE ATTENDED SINCE LAST JUNE.

SUBJECT: "God's Plan for the Family"

10. I thought the class topic was interesting.

(agree)   1   2   3   4   5   6   7   (disagree)

11. The material was difficult to understand.

(agree)   1   2   3   4   5   6   7   (disagree)

12. More time should have been spent in lecture.

(agree)   1   2   3   4   5   6   7   (disagree)

13. More time should have been spent in discussion.

(agree)   1   2   3   4   5   6   7   (disagree)

14. The teacher's apparent knowledge in subject taught was good.

(agree)   1   2   3   4   5   6   7   (disagree)

15. The teacher was always prepared for class.

(agree)   1   2   3   4   5   6   7   (disagree)

16. The teacher was interested and enthusiastic in the subject.

(agree)   1   2   3   4   5   6   7   (disagree)

17. The teacher was able to convey meaning of subject matter well.

(agree)   1   2   3   4   5   6   7   (disagree)

18. The teacher was open to new ideas.

(agree)   1   2   3   4   5   6   7   (disagree)

19. The teacher was a good leader.

(agree)   1   2   3   4   5   6   7   (disagree)

20. My general evaluation of the teacher is excellent.

(agree)   1   2   3   4   5   6   7   (disagree)

21. This teacher rates very high in comparison to other teachers.

(agree)   1   2   3   4   5   6   7   (disagree)

22. My general evaluation of this class is excellent.

(agree)   1   2   3   4   5   6   7   (disagree)

23. This course rates very high in comparison to others.

    (agree)   1   2   3   4   5   6   7   (disagree)

24. I would recommend this teacher to my friends.

    (agree)   1   2   3   4   5   6   7   (disagree)

25. I would recommend this class to my friends.

    (agree)   1   2   3   4   5   6   7   (disagree)

26. I would recommend this teacher for this course.

    (agree)   1   2   3   4   5   6   7   (disagree)

27. It is important that this class is offered.

    (agree)   1   2   3   4   5   6   7   (disagree)

28. The bible could have been used more in this class.

    (agree)   1   2   3   4   5   6   7   (disagree)

29. I benefited intellectually from this class.

    (agree)   1   2   3   4   5   6   7   (disagree)

30. I benefited spiritually from this class.

    (agree)   1   2   3   4   5   6   7   (disagree)

31. What aspect of the life of the church do you personally find most helpful?

    _____ Sunday Worship Service   _____ Social fellowship
    _____ Sermons   _____ None
    _____ Music programs   _____ Other (specify)
                                    _____

32. What do you consider to be the major strengths of the adult Sunday School program?

33. What do you consider to be the major weakness of the adult Sunday School program?

34. What recommendations would you suggest for improving the adult Sunday School program?

35. What would you like to see taught next year?

In order for us to make use of the materials you have completed, we need a little information concerning you. This will be confidential and is for purposes of statistical tabulation only. Check appropriate categories or write in the necessary answers.

36. What is your age? _____   Male_____   Female _____

37. What is the highest level of education you have attained?
    Grade School _____   College Degree _____   Other _____

    High School _____   Graduate Degree _____

38. Present Employment Status:

        Employed   _____   Housewife _____
        Self-employed _____   Student   _____
        Unemployed   _____   Retired   _____

39. If you are employed or self-employed, what kind of work do you do
    (or position held)? _____
    _____

40. What is your home zip code? _____

41. How long have you been attending first united methodist church?
    1 yr. _____   1-10 yrs. _____   10-20 yrs. _____   20-30 yrs. _____
    30 yrs. _____

42. How often do you attend the morning worship service?

    Never   1-10   At least   At least   At least   Almost
    attended   times a   1 mo. _____   2 mo. _____   3 mo. _____   always
    _____   yr. _____   _____

43. Which service do you usually attend?
    9:50 _____   10:50 _____

44. How often do you attend both the morning service and Sunday School?
    Always _____   Most of the time _____   Some of the time _____
    Never _____

45. What is your marital status?
    Single _____   Married _____   Divorced _____   Other _____

46. Please classify yourself as one of these three types of christians:

    _____ Traditional: Stresses the importance of RITUAL
                              concerning Christian practice as
                              governed by the HISTORICAL and defined
                              AUTHORITY of the Church.

    _____ Evangelical: Stresses the importance of PREACHING,
                              emphasizing SALVATION through faith in
                              the death of Jesus Christ through
                              personal conversion and SHARING this
                              faith with others.

    _____ Charismatic: Stresses the importance of SPIRITUAL
                              RENEWAL of power (as of healing) given
                              a Christian by the HOLY SPIRIT for the
                              good of the Church.

47. Which five of the following would you choose as the marks of a
    mature Christian? Place (1) to the left of the most important, (2)
    at the left of the next most important and so on to (5).

<u>Do not mark more than five and do not mark any equally</u>. If you
have items of your own not covered in this list, add them at the
bottom and give them a number among your five choices.

<u>Do not number more than five</u> including any you write in. We regard
all of these as important marks of a Christian. You are to choose
among these really important things those which are the five most
important to you.

These Questions test for 3 types of Christians:
1. Experiential
2. Doctrinal
3. Institutional

_____ 1. Belonging to the Church

_____ 2. Have a correct belief about God

_____ 3. Loving and serving his fellow man

_____ 4. Having a correct belief about the Bible

_____ 5. Engaging in personal prayer

_____ 6. Obeying his ecclesiastical superiors

_____ 7. Having a conscious experience of
fellowship with God

_____ 8. Giving to the church

_____ 9. Having a correct belief about Jesus

_____ 10. Teaching his children the right things
to believe

_____ 11. Living joyfully from day to day

_____ 12. Receiving the sacraments regularly

_____ 13. Having a right belief about life after
death

_____ 14. Remaining confident amid distress and
difficulty

_____ 15. Attending church services regularly

TV EVANGELIST SURVEY

Hello, I'm _____, and I'm from _____, an opinion
research company in _____. We are conducting a nationwide
opinion survey for a well-known TV ministry in order to assist them
in being even more responsive to the needs of the viewing public.
I would like to ask you a few questions about your opinions toward
religious organizations and their importance in your life. Your
answers will be kept confidential and will be used only to determine
general trends among the attitudes of those folks we survey. There

are no right or wrong answers so your frank and candid opinions are
very important.   If at any time you don't understand a question,
stop me and I'll gladly repeat the question.
----

1. Which, if any, of the following religious TV programs have you
   watched in the last 30 days? (READ LIST IN GRID BELOW UNDER "TV
   MINISTRIES AND CIRCLE APPROPRIATE NUMBER UNDER "Q1").

TV MINISTRIES	Q1	Q2	Q3	Q4
Billy Graham	1	1	1	1
Oral Roberts	2	2	2	2
Robert Schuller (Hour of Power)	3	3	3	3
Jerry Falwell (Old Time Gospel Hour)	4	4	4	4
Jimmy Swaggart	5	5	5	5
Richard DeHahn (Day of Discovery)	6	6	6	6
(700 Club)	7	7	7	7
None	0	0	0	0

2. Of these same TV ministries, which have you written a letter to
   in the last 30 days?   (RE-READ LIST IN GRID AND CIRCLE
   APPROPRIATE NUMBER UNDER "Q2")

3. Of these TV ministries mentioned, which program meets your needs
   better than any other? (RE-READ LIST IF NECESSARY AND CIRCLE
   APPROPRIATE NUMBER UNDER "Q3")

4. Of these television ministries, which, if any, have you
   contributed money to in the last year?   (RE-READ LIST IF
   NECESSARY AND CIRCLE APPROPRIATE NUMBER UNDER "Q4")

5. How often do you watch religious TV programming? (READ CHOICES,
   CIRCLE APPROPRIATE NUMBER)

   1 Several times a week   4 Several times a year

   2 Once a week   5 Never

   3 Once a month

6. Now, thinking back to the last 30 days, how many Sundays did you
   watch a televised religious program? (WAIT FOR RESPONSE BEFORE
   READING CHOICES, THEN CIRCLE APPROPRIATE NUMBER.)

   1 1 time   4 4 times

   2 2 times   5 0 times

   3 3 times

7. As I read the following statements regarding religious television programs, tell me whether you, strongly agree, somewhat agree, somewhat disagree, or strongly disagree. (READ CHOICES, 1, STRONGLY AGREE, 2, SOMEWHAT AGREE, 3, SOMEWHAT DISAGREE, 4, STRONGLY DISAGREE. DON'T READ DON'T KNOW!!)

	Strongly Agree	Somewhat Agree	Somewhat Disagree	Strongly Disagree	DON'T KNOW
a. The donations are always spent for worthy projects.	1	2	3	4	(5)
b. Religious TV programs ask for money too often.	1	2	3	4	(5)
c. Television evangelists answer your letters in a personal manner.	1	2	3	4	(5)
d. These programs have too many write-in gimmicks.	1	2	3	4	(5)
e. TV evangelists really help you with your spiritual needs.	1	2	3	4	(5)
f. Some programs are becoming too "hollywood" or polished.	1	2	3	4	(5)
g. The sermons and teachings could be improved.	1	2	3	4	(5)
h. Their emphasis has shifted too much from the spititual to entertainment	1	2	3	4	(5)
i. Fund raising by TV ministries through telethons is a good idea.	1	2	3	4	(5)
j. TV ministries send out too much mail.	1	2	3	4	(5)
k. Giving money to religious causes is more important than giving to any other cause.	1	2	3	4	(5)

1. TV evangelists do
   not use donations
   for personal gain.   1   2   3   4   (5)

---

8. What could TV ministries do to better meet your needs?

9. During the past six months what percent of your total income
   did you contribute to religious TV ministries? (READ CHOICES
   AND CIRCLE)

   1 Less than 1%   5 None

   2 1 to 4%   6 REFUSED

   3 5 to 9%   7 DON'T KNOW

   4 10% or more

10. Please complete this statement: I would give more money to TV
    ministries if:

11. How many Sundays, in the past 30 days, did you attend a church
    service at your local church?   (WAIT FOR RESPONSE BEFORE
    READING CHOICES AND CIRCLE APPROPRIATE NUMBER).

    1 1 time   4 4 times

    2 2 times   5 0 times

    3 3 times   6 DON'T KNOW

12. During the past six months what percent of your total income
    did you contribute to the church of your choice?   (READ
    CHOICES)

    1 Less than 1%   4 10% or more

    2 1 to 4%   5 None

    3 5 to 9%   6 REFUSED

           7 DON'T KNOW

13. If you were to give money to a charitable organization, how would you rank these in order of importance, i.e., 1=most important, 2=second most important, etc. WRITE IN 1 THRU 6) (ROTATE) (READ CHOICES)

    Religious TV _____   Churches   _____

    United Way _____   Overseas Mission _____

    Health Organizations_____ Don't Know _____

14. Which of the following best describes your employment status? (CIRCLE APPROPRIATE NUMBER).

    1 Full time   5 Homemaker

    2 Part time   6 Unemployed, currently
    3 Retired   between jobs

    4 Student   7 Other

              8 REFUSED

15. Are you: 1 Married   (READ CHOICES)

             2 Widowed

             3 Separated

             4 Remarried

             5 Divorced

             6 Single

             7 REFUSED

16. Which of the following age categories do you fall within? (READ CHOICES)

    1 18 to 34   4 65 or older

    2 35 to 49   5 REFUSED

    3 50 to 64

17. Which of the following best describes your church preference? (READ CHOICES)

    1 Roman Catholic   5 Lutheran

    2 Jewish   6 Interdenominational

    3 Baptist   7 Other (SPECIFY) _____

    4 Methodist   8 REFUSED

18. Which of the following income categories best describes your total household income before taxes? (CIRCLE APPROPRIATE NUMBER AND STATE THAT THEIR NAMES ARE NOT KEPT AND THAT THE INFORMATION IS GROUPED)

    1 Under 5,000   5 25,000 or more

    2 5,000 to 10,000   6 REFUSED

    3 10,000 to 15,000   7 DON'T KNOW

    4 15,000 to 25,000

19. Have you ever made a personal commitment to Jesus Christ?

    1 Yes (GO TO 20)

    2 No (THANK YOU AND TERMINATE)

    3 Don't Know (THANK YOU AND TERMINATE)

20. Is that commitment still important today?

    1 Yes (GO TO 21)

    2 No (THANK YOU AND TERMINATE)

    3 Don't Know (THANK YOU AND TERMINATE)

21. Do you feel that your commitment to Jesus Christ was a turning point in your life?

    1 Yes

    2 No

    3 Don't Know

Name _____ City _____
     (only for validation)

Phone No. _____ Interviewer's Initials _____

Appendix B:
Sample Marketing Plans

MARKETING PLAN FOR A CHURCH
Pine Grove Church
Monroe, Louisiana

Introduction

This plan was developed for Pine Grove Church, Inc., a local full gospel church in Monroe, Louisiana. Pine Grove Church, Inc. concentrates on reaching Monroe, West Monroe, and the Ouachita Parish area with the gospel of Jesus Christ. Its vision also includes supporting missions and missionaries around the world. Pine Grove Church, Inc. (PGC) also operates Pine Grove Christian Academy (PGCA), a Bible-based school program for Kindergarten through 12th grade. All of the funds for the church operation are received through donations, gifts and fundraisers. School funds are provided through tuition. The school is underwritten by the church.

Executive Summary

Environment

The population of Ouachita Parish is estimated at 146,000. Monroe population is 56,600 and West Monroe is 14,500. Monroe is a college town and Pine Grove Church is located only one mile from Northeast Louisiana University (NLU), so there is a large college population that is a good opportunity. There are a wide variety of denominational churches as well as full gospel churches in the area. However, PGC is one of the best known and largest in the area.

Strategy Summary

Pine Grove Church will implement a grow and build strategy. Growth will include all aspects of the church and the school and the strategy will concentrate on establishing the needed income to finance the future growth. Some of the ways to accomplish this will be: (1) to call the church to pray and fast; (2) to inform and challenge constituents to increase their giving; (3) to challenge the people to increase missions giving, which will, in turn, increase church income and; (4) to increase attendance by encouraging constituents to invite others and reach out to the community. Constituent needs will be better met by establishing a plan that will begin with a questionnaire to be approved by the deacons and sent out to all members.

Financial Impact

The analysis of revenues and costs reveals that approximately $315,000 is required annually to maintain the present operations. An estimated $500,000 annual budget and zero indebtedness will be necessary before construction begins on any new facilities.

Marketing Opportunities

1. Opportunity for Pine Grove Church to reach out to students on the NLU campus and encourage them to come.
2. Opportunity for each youth group and Sunday School class to reach out to the community and bring in more people.
3. Opportunity for PGCA to advertise the school program and interest more families in the school.
4. Opportunity for PGC to support and/or sponsor additional missionaries or other organizations.
5. Opportunity for PGC to reach out to the elderly community. Transportation could be provided to the church.
6. Opportunity to encourage the body to get more involved in the available activities.
7. Opportunity to advertise the available activities to the public.

Potential Benefits

1. Expand each group within PGC, thus expanding the church's impact on the community.
2. Create a greater awareness of PGC.
3. Become affiliated with other ministries world-wide through missionary efforts.
4. Draw more people to all available advertised activities, thus reaching more people with the gospel.

Objectives

Ministry (Short-Term Goals)

   I. Church
      A. Increase Sunday morning attendance by 20 percent.
      B. Increase constituent giving by 10 percent.
      C. Institute a plan to determine constituent needs.

  II. J-Team (Jr. High Youth Group)
      A. Increase average attendance from 10-30.
      B. Offer new activities that will encourage new members.
      C. Reach out to the community and area junior high schools.
      D. Encourage current members to invite friends.

 III. SNL & Alpha Omega (High School and College Youth Groups)
      A. Increase average attendance from 50-100.
      B. Maintain personal contact with each member.
      C. Provide activities and spiritual ministry of the Word and the Holy Spirit through teaching and counseling.
      D. Offer camp retreats and special services to help and appeal to young people.
      E. Establish a self-perpetuating, self-sustaining youth movement for instilling Christian character in young leaders.
      F. Meet spiritual, physical, and emotional needs of members by the gifts of the Spirit.
      G. Increase staff in proportion to membership increases.

IV. Single Again (Singles Group over 30)
   A. To obtain 100 percent growth by the end of the year.
   B. To encourage intergroup friendships.
   C. To develop spiritually, independently, and emotionally.
   D. To be more involved in community affairs.
   E. To participate in and begin outreach missions.
   F. To turn the emphasis from singleness to the possibilities of a Christian walk.
   G. To continue to be involved in retreats and singles conferences.

 V. Sunday School (Includes all age groups)
   A. To encourage each class to be more active individually.
   B. To keep the church informed of the different classes, teachers, and activities. To boost interest in the classes.
   C. To encourage growth of up to 30 percent.

VI. Music
   A. To lead the body of Christ into the presence of God in a time set aside as worship.
   B. To encourage greater involvement of musicians and choir in worship.
   C. To maintain and purchase musical equipment as needed.
   D. To designate responsibilities as needed.
   E. To maintain quality relationships with musicians.
   F. To prepare for worship service with prayer and Bible study.

VII. Children's Church
   A. Increase membership by 20 percent.
   B. Recruit more volunteers to serve on the staff.
   C. Consider the possibilities of a bus ministry to pick up area children.
   D. Maintain personal relationships with all children. (Visit the sick, etc.)
   E. Build puppet stage and use puppets more.

VIII. Facilities (Building)
    A. Functional
        1. Enlarge and completely remodel kitchen.
        2. Build additional storage areas.
        3. Enlarge and improve rear parking.
    B. Beautification
        1. Repair sanctuary, hallways, and fellowship hall.
        2. Install floor tile in foyer.
        3. Blow new ceiling in foyer.
        4. Landscape front of building.
        5. Light building front.
        6. New lighted sign.

IX. PGCA
    A. To increase enrollment by 20 percent.
    B. To maintain personal relationships with all students and their families.
    C. To offer extracurricular activities that will appeal to students.

Strategy

Basic

    I. To position PGC as a full gospel, full-service church offering a wide range of activities for all age groups and interests.
    II. To reach out to the community by advertising, word-of-mouth and personal outreach.
    III. Develop a brochure for visitors to promote church programs.
    IV. Develop a program to specifically define constituents' needs through a survey of members.

Program Strategy

    I. Each separate group and youth organization is to report directly to one of the three pastors.
    II. All volunteers for the separate programs are to report to the group leader who is to report to the pastor.

III. Each program offered should keep the church informed and aware of all activities.

IV. Offer a full range of programs for all age groups of various compositions, based on analysis of each group's needs.

Contributions Strategy

I. Keep the constituents informed of church finances and needs through quarterly business meetings.

II. Encourage constituents to tithe regularly by showing the biblical basis for it.

III. Emphasize giving for local church needs as well as to other ministries and missionaries.

IV. Seek endowment for PGCA to support expansion of the school.

Communications Strategy

I. In-house Communication

  A. Construct in the church office a wall/cabinet/shelf with boxes for the mail, memos, and other information for each department, staff member, and group. Each person responsible for the group should check the box for communications.

  B. Construct two new bulletin boards and keep them current, attractive, and informative with all church activities.

  C. Place all announcements in the weekly bulletin to be given at the Sunday morning worship service.

II. Other Communications

  A. An annual calendar will be developed to plan events, speakers, and functions. This will help in planning advertising in advance for such events.

  B. Communication of church events will be done by utilizing *free* public service announcements on radio and possibly in the newspaper.

  C. Posters will be made (handouts) and placed in local businesses to announce activities and invite the public to attend.

    D. Church brochure will be developed to provide information about church, staff, group activities, etc. The brochure will be given to new members, visitors, and other interested parties, and also placed at the Monroe Tourism Bureau.

    E. Purchase advertising space to advertise the school and other programs in the local newspaper.

    F. A bumper sticker campaign will be used to promote the church in the local area. (I ♥ Pine Grove)

Access Strategy

    I. Initial contact will be made through advertising or by visiting the church.

    II. After the visit, a follow-up letter will be sent in response to the visitor's card. They will be contacted by the group to which they would belong.

    III. Individuals will be given an opportunity to join the church one Sunday a month.

    IV. Regular services will be offered on Sunday morning, Sunday evening and Wednesday evening.

    V. Special services and activities will be offered by various groups within the church to provide access to services at other times.

Plan Controls

The following control procedures will be established:

1. Evaluate the tithes and offerings received at the end of each month after implementing the plan comparing budgeted amounts with receipts.
2. Evaluate enrollment figures on an annual basis in each group.
3. Evaluate staff members and staff needs to make sure an adequate number of well-trained staff is maintained.
4. Evaluate advertising efforts. Determine where and how new members learned of Pine Grove through a survey of new members.

MARKETING PLAN FOR A MINISTRY

Introduction

This plan was developed for a missionary outreach program headquartered on the Texas-Mexico border. The missionary effort concentrated on bringing Mexican nationals into a Bible training program which lasted 18 months. Graduates were then encouraged to return to areas in Mexico where no churches existed and build a church/congregation. Most of the funds for this operation were provided by friends, relatives and others who had learned about the mission work. No formal planning existed prior to the development of this plan.

Executive Summary

Environment

The environment and statistics show that the population of Mexico was estimated at 69,965,000 in the 1980 census, and is expected to continue to grow at a rate of 2.6 percent until 1986, when the growth rate is expected to drop to 2.4 percent. Computations also show that 89 percent of the population is Catholic, and 77 percent are still married in the church. Also, 80 percent of the population was estimated to be literate. This data shows there is a large literate population that has had some contact with the Christian message, and thus Mexico should be considered a prime mission ground.

Objectives

The short-range objectives are to graduate 15 students and have them start at least two new churches a year. Also, trips to raise support should begin with no less than two successful contacts each month the school is not in session. The long-range objectives are to enroll 35 new students a year, graduate 20-25 students a year, have these graduates start a minimum of three churches a year, and begin enrolling married couples in the school. Also included in the long-range objectives are to use money generated from the sponsor trips to build needed facilities and to be able to train a greater number of students. Another long-range objective is to hire a dependable graduate to take sponsor trips into American churches on a larger scale.

Strategy Summary

The strategy to establish the needed income for continued growth of Border Ministries will be to use a personal contact technique in various churches to raise missionary support. This will be done by contacting churches, planning to visit two or three a month, and using a well-aimed presentation and slide show to gain these churches' support for the ministry. The aim will be to get the churches to regularly support a few students through a scholarship fund and to contribute to a long-range building project fund. Another long-range strategic aim is to get churches personally involved by sending American teams from supporting churches to the mission to work on location for a week.

The potential benefits of getting churches involved with the ministry through the scholarship fund, the building fund, and mission teams will be to achieve the desired long-range results of a dependable future income necessary for continued growth.

Financial Impact

The analysis of revenues and costs reveals that approximately $50,000 is required annually to maintain the present operations. A $1,500 incremental cost is associated with each student supported by the scholarship fund, and an estimated $60,000 is needed in the building fund to begin construction.

Constituent Analysis

Giving

Giving is defined as "committing the trust or keeping of another for a definite purpose by an act of will." According to the Bible, giving is a responsibility (Duet. 14:28-29), and hoarding wealth should be subservient to giving, for "no one can serve two masters . . ." (Matt. 6:24). God has put money at our disposal, but the implication is that we have the responsibility to use money within God's plan. Also, in Christ's parable of the talents in Matt. 25,

Christ seems to be stressing the importance of handling money judiciously. This shows that the steward is responsible for the money he is entrusted with—for how well it is used, and for the kind of spiritual return it will bring for Christ's glorification. "Giving" in the world's sense is an act of will, but God considers giving a responsibility through which we will learn and practice integrity and good stewardship (I Chron. 29:14-17).

Individual donors in the United States have historically provided 83 percent of all funds given in philanthropy. Corporations and businesses contributed about 7 percent, and foundations another 10 percent. Private philanthropy in the United States in 1980 totaled over 60 billion.

In the area of religious giving, the percentage contrast of total contributions made by individual donors versus corporate giving becomes even more extreme. Less than one percent of the $18.4 billion of private philanthropy that was directed to religion in 1978 came from foundations. Almost without exception, the total amount given to religious causes came from individuals, and the total amount given to religion accounted for nearly half (46 percent) of all philanthropy to charities of any variety.

Religious giving constitutes almost half of all charitable contributions in the United States. A great opportunity, then, exists for us if a proper marketing strategy is formed to effectively reach a portion of the market share and obtain funds for the Institute. The opportunities available to the ministry presently are:

1. Opportunity for Border Ministries to appeal mainly to charismatic Christians and churches.
2. Opportunity for Border Ministries to expand its spiritual impact in Mexico.
3. Opportunity for charismatic churches to become involved and affiliated with Border Ministries.

Marketing Opportunities

1. Opportunity for charismatic churches to sponsor a student through seminary.
2. Opportunity for charismatic churches to sponsor the satellite churches started by graduates.

3. Opportunity for sponsorship to the completion of the planned building project needed for continued growth.

Potential Benefits

1. Opportunity to expand its spiritual impact on the surrounding society.
2. Opportunity of charismatic churches to become affiliated and involved with Border Ministries.
3. Opportunity to create greater awareness of Border Ministries throughout the U.S.

Objectives

Ministry

   I. One-Year Goals
     A. Graduate 15 students.
     B. Have graduates start two new churches.
  II. Three- to Five-Year Goals
     A. Enroll 35 new students per year.
     B. Graduate 20-25 students per year.
     C. Have graduates start three new churches per year.
     D. Enroll married couples in the training program.
     E. Have church services in new chapel with Sunday School.
     F. Have children's programs in new chapel.

Facilities

   I. One-Year Goals
     A. Remodel Kitchen.
      1. Install new cabinets.
      2. Buy dishwasher and install.
      3. Buy new refrigerator.
     B. New Parsonage.
      1. Tear down old buildings.
      2. Build one new home.
      3. Create new bathroom.
     C. Remodel Bathrooms and Men's Dormitory.
      1. Tile floors of bathroom.

    2. Buy new foam mattress pads.
    3. Tile dormitories.
    4. Buy new desks for replacement.
II. Three- to Five-Year Goals
  A. New Chapel on Lot North of Institute.
    1. Build chapel to hold 400 people.
    2. Build Sunday School facilities.
  B. New Men's Dormitories.
    1. Remodel old chapel to use as dormitory.
    2. Refurnish dormitories.
  C. Build Apartments for Married Couples.
    1. Build one-bedroom efficiency apartments on same lot as new chapel.
    2. Complete ten apartments.

Fundraising

I. One- to Three-Year Goals
  A. Establish scholarship fund.
  B. Establish building fund.
  C. Send letters to 60-75 prospective churches.
  D. Visit 12-20 churches that responded.
  E. Use slide show for presentation.
  F. Create newsletter to be sent to donors.
  G. Emphasize scholarship fund primarily in this period.
    1. Have cost of sending student for year available.
    2. Invite sponsor churches to visit the Institute.
  H. Involve graduate assistant in recruiting process.
II. Three- to Five-Year Goals
  A. Continue scholarship program with excess into building fund.
  B. Hire a fulltime recruiter/accountant.
    1. Will travel to churches.
    2. Keep books, expenditures and receipts.
  C. Emphasize building fund heavily in this period.
  D. Invite sponsor churches to visit building sites.
  E. Increase printings of newsletter from two to four times a year.

Strategy

Basic

I. Write and send letters to potential supporting churches to develop a promotional schedule.
II. Develop and include brochure with introductory letter to potential supporting churches. Include in the brochure:
   A. Brief history
   B. Short biography on founder
   C. Ministry's purpose
   D. Description of facilities
   E. Pictures of founder, facilities, students
   F. Explanation of needs
   G. Objectives for future
   H. Opportunity for giving
   I. Address and phone number
III. Develop and use slide show that presents both the financial needs of the students and the financial needs for building.

Program Strategy

I. Present an opportunity to give into an ongoing, productive ministry.
II. Pass out pledge cards at the beginning of a service, and keep in contact with those that respond with a monthly newsletter that describes the ongoing actions, needs and opportunities of the ministry.
III. If a church or an individual contributes a large sum of money, give them an honorary plaque. If they sponsor part of a building project, name a wing or hall after them. If they agree to sponsor an entire building project, name the entire project after them.
IV. Each family at the beginning of the service should receive a pledge card. This card should read something like "I pledge to support Border Ministries with $10 15 25 50 100 150 (circle one) a month." Also on the card is room to mark a one-time donation, and a place for the individual's address.

Contributions Strategy

  I. Establish a Scholarship Fund based on the results of the pledge cards; if an individual pledges $10-5,000 a year for scholarships, designate this pledge for the scholarship fund.
  II. If an individual or church pledges over $5,000 a year, generally designate these incoming monies for a Building Fund.
  III. For undesignated pledges under $5,000, use these pledges in a General Fund for operational needs.

Communications Strategy

  I. To get invited for promotional visits to churches, send an introductory letter and a brochure that tells about the ministry. If no response, send another letter without the brochure, and call the church a few days after the second letter should arrive.
  II. In the presentation, show the two distinct needs of a scholarship fund and a building fund in a slide show. The first half of the presentation should show the needs of the culture of your pastors, and the second half should show the need for the ministry's physical expansion.
  III. At the end of the presentation, let the pastor of the church take an offering, and be sure to retrieve the pledge cards in the offering.
  IV. Within a week of receiving new pledges, send a newsletter to the recently-visited church and to the individuals that have pledged.

Access Strategy

  I. Direct mail will be the initial contact.
  II. Response from the direct mail piece will prompt an invitation.
  III. When a pledge is made, a newsletter should go to the pledging church or individual.

Ministry Financial Needs

All the financial resources of the ministry are based on gifts from people who are familiar with the work, friends of the founder, and a small salary for the founder as an appointed missionary for the Church of the Apostles. Currently it costs $1,500 per student per year at Border Ministries. Current enrollment ranges from 20 to 25 students per year.

There are also building costs that need to be covered. The current estimates are as follows:

Chapel Auditorium	$ 75,000
Married Housing	30,000
Director's Housing	5,000
Total Building Needs	$110,000

Current operating expenses are estimated at $50,000 per year, with the present enrollment of 25 students. The short-term objective is to expand to 35 students. It is estimated this would raise operating expenses to approximately $65,000 per year. Given this figure, construction should begin once $30,000 is escrowed for construction. This would allow construction to begin on the married housing units, which cost $5,000 per unit.

Plan Controls

The following control procedures should be established:

1. Evaluate the number of pledges received and the annual amount pledged at the end of each quarter after implementing the plan.
2. Evaluate total contributions related to the marketing plan (above what was normally received) on a quarterly basis.
3. Contact pastors two weeks after each presentation to get their input on how to improve the presentation, and also to maintain contact with these pastors.
4. Evaluate enrollment figures on an annual basis, noting deviations from planned enrollments.
5. Evaluate students' and contributors' attitudes toward the ministry on an annual basis.

Index